AUTHENTIC TRANSCRIPTIONS WITH NOTES AND TABLATURE

# ROBERT JOHNSON

## *The New Transcriptions*

Music transcriptions by Pete Billmann

Robert Johnson photo booth self-portrait, ca. early 1930s


ISBN 978-0-7935-8919-7

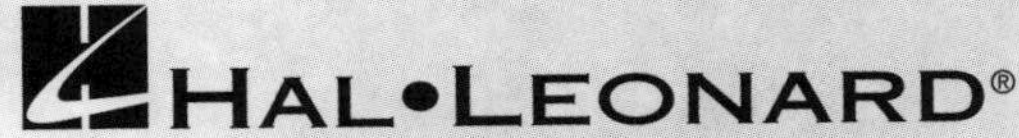




Contact Us:
**Hal Leonard**
7777 West Bluemound Road
Milwaukee, WI 53213
Email: info@halleonard.com

In Europe contact:
**Hal Leonard Europe Limited**
Distribution Centre, Newmarket Road
Bury St Edmunds, Suffolk, IP33 3YB
Email: info@halleonardeurope.com

In Australia contact:
**Hal Leonard Australia Pty. Ltd.**
4 Lentara Court
Cheltenham, Victoria, 3192 Australia
Email: info@halleonard.com.au

# ROBERT JOHNSON

## *The New Transcriptions*

# ROBERT JOHNSON

## *The Greatest Blues Guitarist*

1911-1938

In the history of American popular music, there have been a handful of certifiable instrumental geniuses: Louis Armstrong, Charlie Christian, Art Tatum, Charlie Parker, John Coltrane, and Jimi Hendrix among them. With this publication of *Robert Johnson: The New Transcriptions*, following on the heels of the several box sets released in the nineties, this exalted group should be increased by one. Robert Johnson's monumental contribution to blues, and by extension R&B and rock 'n' roll confirms his place among the aforementioned giants.

The fascinating facts and myths of Johnson's life are still being sorted out. It is the stuff of melodramatic fiction and may yet make it to the silver screen. His music, however, lives with us in various audio formats and now, for the first time, accurately on paper. To arrive at this point has been no easy task. Over two years of listening, studying, and researching historical documentation by several experts in their field has yielded this: *the* authoritative Robert Johnson transcription collection. Presented here in their entirety are all twenty-nine songs plus an alternate take of "Phonograph Blues" and the recently-discovered "Traveling Riverside Blues" (Take 1). As several versions (takes) of many songs exist, we have referenced each of the transcriptions by the matrix number of Johnson's original recording (i.e. "Kind Hearted Woman Blues" SA 2580-1) so that you will be able to identify which take has been transcribed. In addition, the songs are presented in the order in which they were recorded, rather than in alphabetical order. In this way, you will be able to better understand Johnson's thought process as he moved from song to song and from one tuning to the next.

Since all modern-day transcriptions have used the old LPs or CD box sets for their audio source, there has always been speculation as to the true keys and tunings. The songs in this book have been transcribed using the original 78s from Johnson archivist Steve LaVere's collection. Surprisingly, perhaps, the 78s have a much higher fidelity, affording us the ability to hear previously muted notes as well as to assess the actual keys that Johnson used. (To hear for yourself, obtain the 1998 reissue of *The King of The Delta Blues Singers'*, Sony/Columbia CK/CT 65745.) The result of all these factors is a book containing extremely detailed note-for-note transcriptions. As you study and play through the songs, you will discover, as we have, several unique playing techniques and tunings that eluded Johnson's contemporaries, not to mention all the guitarists who have attempted to play his music.

Johnson had several musical themes that he employed during his short career. Looking at his repertoire from this point of view is a good way to first approach it. "Kind Hearted Woman Blues" Take 1 (SA 2580-1), which contains his only recorded solo, is like "Phonograph Blues" Take 1 (SA 2587-1), "Dead Shrimp Blues" (SA 2628-2), "Me and The Devil Blues" (DAL 398-1), and "Honeymoon Blues" (DAL 401-1). The boogie rhythm of "I Believe I'll Dust My Broom" (SA 2581-1) is recycled in "Phonograph Blues" Take 2 (SA 2587-2) and is also the basis for "Sweet Home Chicago" (SA 2582-1) and "When You Got a Good Friend" (SA 2584-1). In addition, a variation on this theme appears in "Ramblin' on My Mind" (SA 2583-1), a song that contains slide, as opposed to the other boogie tunes. The format for "Terraplane Blues" (SA 2586-1) shows up again in "Stones in My Passway" (DAL 377-2). Lastly, "If I Had Possession over Judgment Day" (SA 2633-1) is similar to "Traveling Riverside Blues" (DAL 400-2 and 1).

The most exciting result stemming from our research was the discovery of an open tuning apparently without precedent. Called Aadd9 (due to the inclusion of B, the 9th of A), it occurs in "I Believe I'll Dust My Broom" and its sister song, "Phonograph Blues" (Take 2). This tuning is only one whole step away from Open A (see tuning legends under song titles), but functions completely differently. In open A (Johnson's favorite tuning), the root is on string 5 (A). In Aadd9 tuning, the root is on string 6 (E), effecting a whole host of technical considerations, not the least of which is that boogie patterns can be easily played on the two bottom bass strings. Along with this, similar to Open E (and D) tunings, a "blues box" is formed in the open position and at fret 12 (the octave) for the I chord, and at frets 5 and 7 for the IV and V chords, respectively. Within this box, rich blues tones like the ♭7th and ♭5th, not to mention the root, 3rd, and 5th fall easily under the fingers. Most significantly, the main theme, or "hook," of "I Believe I'll Dust My Broom" and "Phonograph Blues" (see the beginning of each verse) can be played in its basic form with one finger. This aspect cannot be overstated, as Johnson relied extensively on barres with his index or middle fingers, as opposed to wrapping his thumb over the edge of the neck like so many other country blues guitarists. (For instance, barres are absolutely required to play the turnarounds, many of which contain subtle harmonies that are tricky to access no matter what the tuning.) For an in-depth discussion of the tunings and techniques employed in each and every song, plese refer to *Robert Johnson: King of the Delta Blues* (HL00660066), a Guitar School book published by Hal Leonard Corporation.

Robert Johnson has long been viewed as a mysterious, tortured artist who composed dark poetic lyrics, sold his soul to the devil at the "crossroads," and was tragically murdered at a young age. This obsession with the legend of his life and death that grips so many fans and journalists has partially obscured the true nature of his accomplishment. Though his work bears comparison to that of his predecessors and contemporaries (guitarists and pianists alike), their music was utterly transformed in his hands, creating a world of blues like no other. And that world still contains secrets to be uncovered. Meanwhile, you now hold in your hands the key to the 61 Highway and beyond.

Dave Rubin
New York City, 1998

# Kind Hearted Woman Blues

**SA 2580 - 1**

**Words and Music by Robert Johnson**

*Tune Down 1/2 Step; Capo II:

① = E♭ ④ = D♭

② = B♭ ⑤ = A♭

③ = G♭ ⑥ = E♭

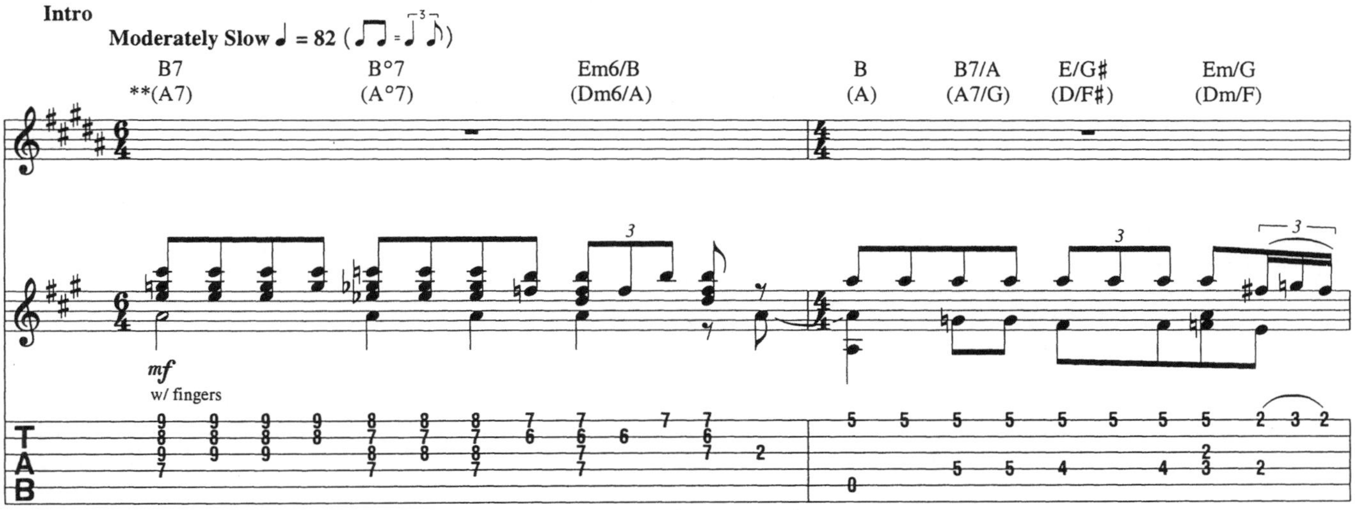

**Intro**

**Moderately Slow ♩ = 82**

B7 **(A7) | B°7 (A°7) | Em6/B (Dm6/A) | B (A) | B7/A (A7/G) | E/G♯ (D/F♯) | Em/G (Dm/F)

*mf*

w/ fingers

**Symbols in parentheses represent chord names (implied tonality) respective to capoed guitar. Symbols above reflect harmony implied by vocals. Capoed fret is "0" in TAB.

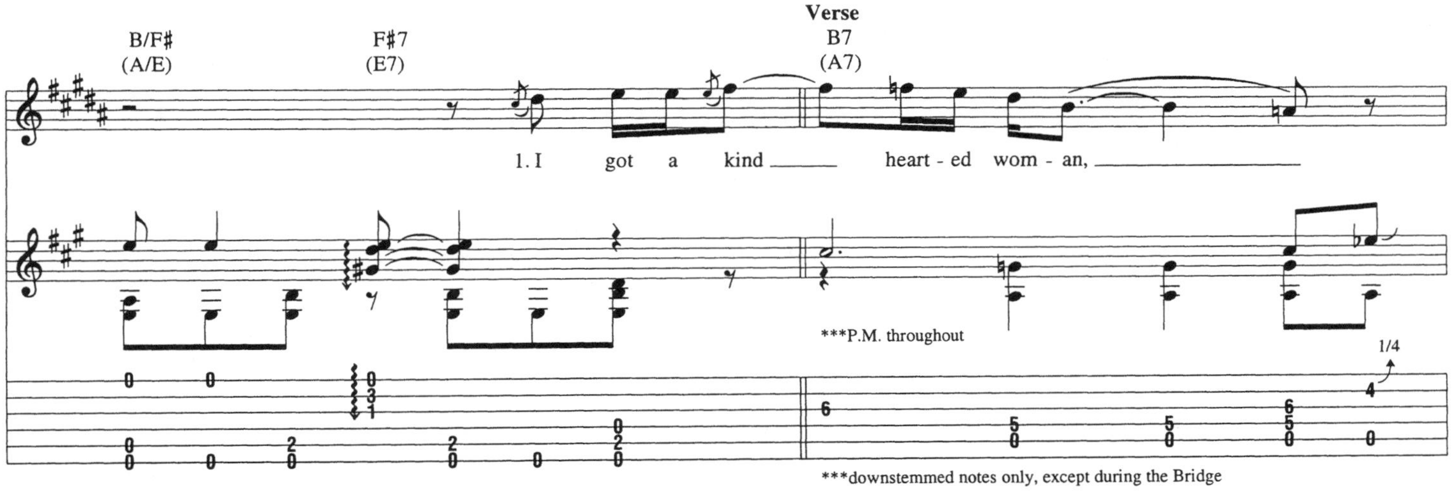

B/F♯ (A/E) | F♯7 (E7)

**Verse**

B7 (A7)

1. I got a kind ___ heart - ed wom - an, ___

***P.M. throughout

1/4

***downstemmed notes only, except during the Bridge

B°7 (A°7)

do an - y - thing'n this world ___ for me. ___

B7 (A7) | B7 (A°7)

*Tunings were determined using the original 78s. To play along with the *Robert Johnson - The Complete Recordings* CD set, Capo III.

B7
(A7)
E7/G#
(D7/F#)
I got a kind heart-ed wom-an,
do an-y-thing'n this world for me.
B7
(A7)
B°7
(A°7)
B7
(A7)
F#7
(E7)
But these e-
vil heart-ed wom-en,
E7/G#
(D7/F#)
man, they will not let me be.
B
(A)
B7/A
(A7/G)
E/G#
(D/F#)
Em/G
(Dm/F)
B/F#
(A/E)
F#7
(E7)
Verse
B7
(A7)
2. I love my ba-by.
My ba-by don't love me.

B°7
(A°7)
B7
(A7)
B°7
(A°7)
B7
(A7)
E7/G#
(D7/F#)
I love my ba - by, oooh.
My ba - by don't love me.
B7
(A7)
B°7
(A°7)
B7
(A7)
I real - ly
F#7
(E7)
love that wom - an,
E7/B
(D7/A)
can't stand to leave her be.
B
(A)
B7/A
(A7/G)
E/G#
(D/F#)
Em/G
(Dm/F)
B/F#
(A/E)
F#7
(E7)
Bridge
B7
(A7)
A - ain't but the one thing

B°7
(A°7)
B7
(A7)
makes Mis-ter John-son drink. I's wor-ried 'bout how you treat me, ba-by.
E7/G♯
(A7/F♯)
I be-gin to think. Oh, babe, my life don't feel the same.
1/2
* P.M.
1/4
* Resume P.M. on downstem notes.
F♯7
(E7)
You breaks my heart when you call
E7/B
(D7/A)
B
(A)
B7/A
(A7/G)
E/G♯
(D/F♯)
Em/G
(Dm/F)
B/F♯
(A/E)
Mis-ter So-and-So's name.

Guitar Solo
B7
(A7)
1/4

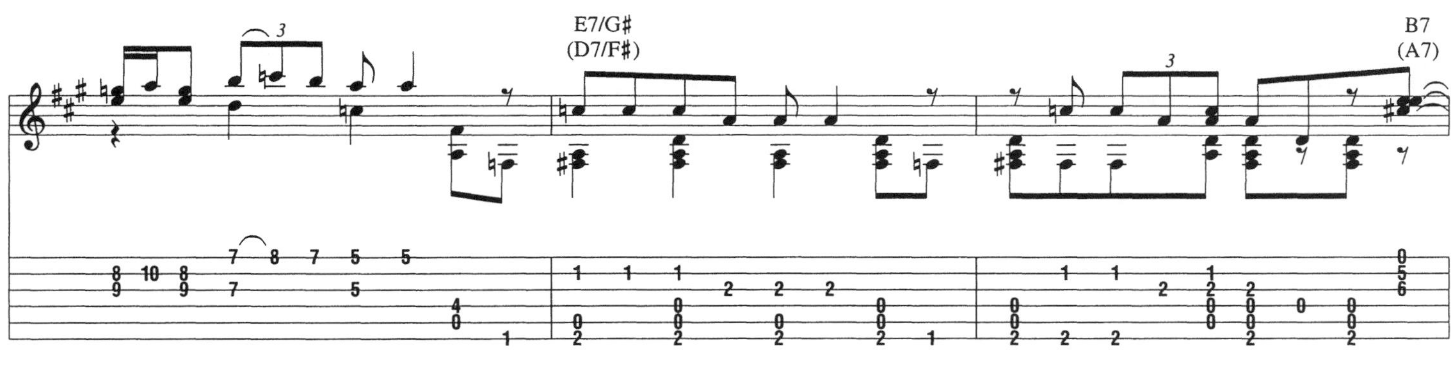
E7/G♯
(D7/F♯)
B7
(A7)

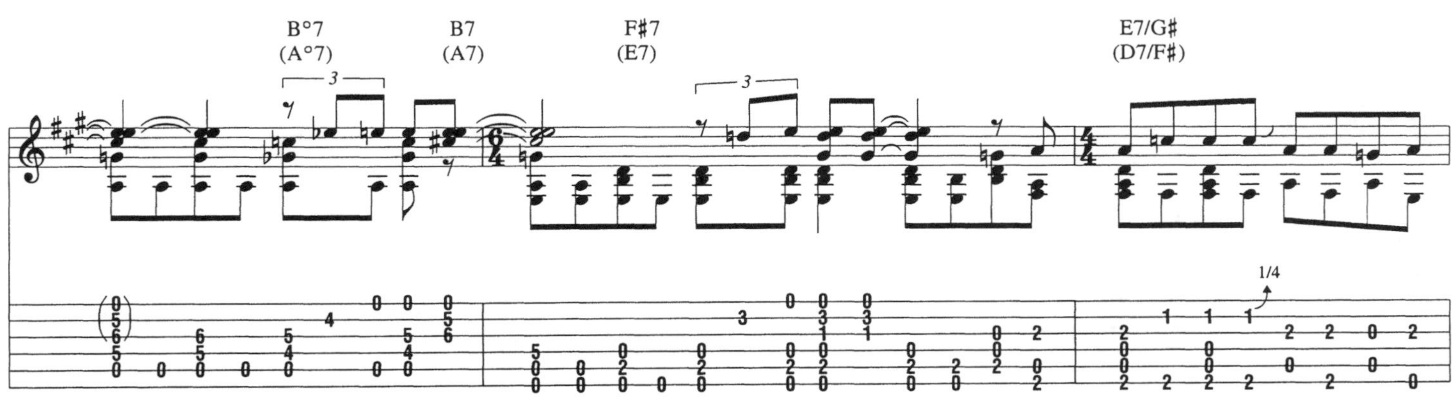
B°7
(A°7)
B7
(A7)
F♯7
(E7)
E7/G♯
(D7/F♯)
1/4

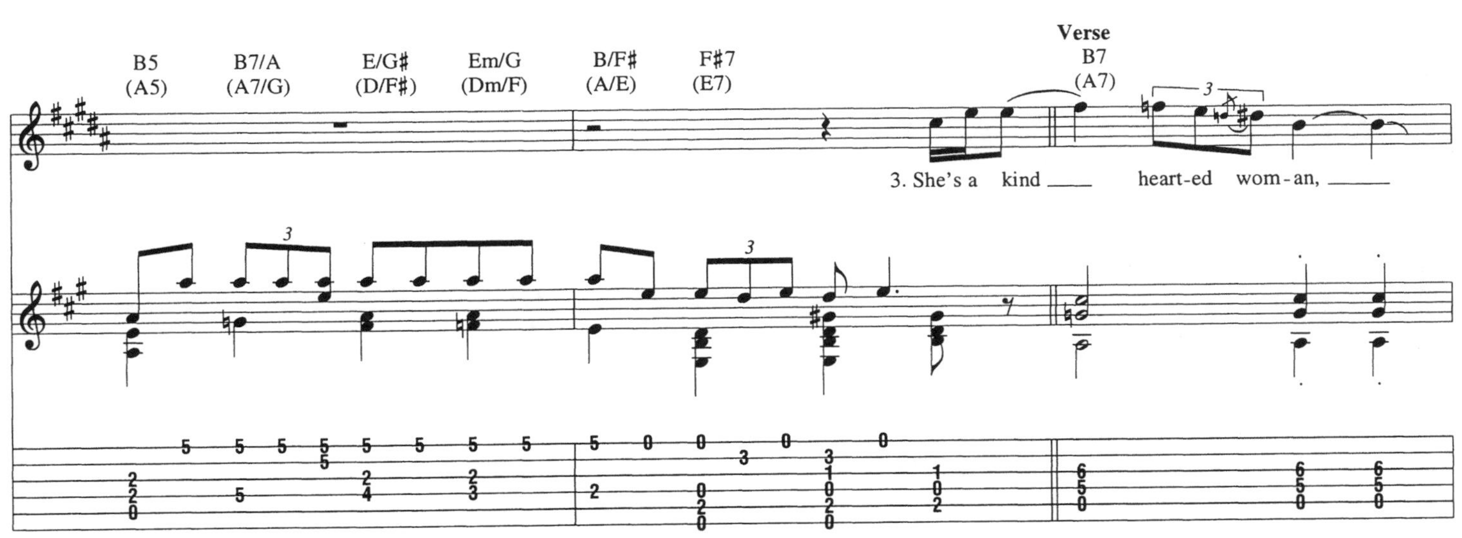
B5
(A5)
B7/A
(A7/G)
E/G♯
(D/F♯)
Em/G
(Dm/F)
B/F♯
(A/E)
F♯7
(E7)
Verse
B7
(A7)
3. She's a kind heart-ed wom-an,

B°7
(A°7)
she stud-ies e - vil all the time.
B7
(A7)
B°7
(A°7)
B7
(A7)
She's a kind
1/4
E7/F#
(D7/F#)
heart - ed wom - an,
she stud - ies e - vil all the time.
B7
(A7)
B°7
(A°7)
B7
(A7)
F#7
(E7)
You well's to kill me,
E7/G#
(D7/A)
B
(A)
B7/A
(A7/G)
E/G#
(D/F#)
Em/G
(Dm/F)
F#7
(E7)
B7
(A7)
as to have it on your mind.

# I Believe I'll Dust My Broom

SA 2581 - 1

Words and Music by Robert Johnson

*Aadd9 Tuning, Down 1/2 Step:
(1) = E♭ (4) = E♭
(2) = C (5) = B♭
(3) = A♭ (6) = E♭

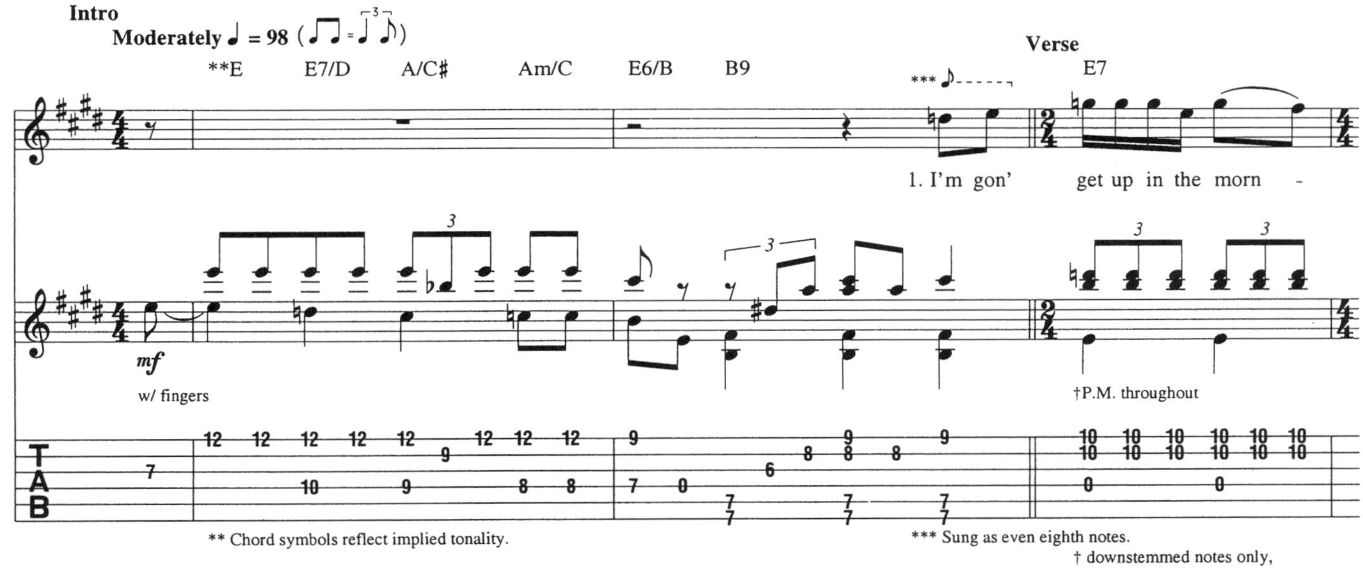


** Chord symbols reflect implied tonality.

*** Sung as even eighth notes.

† downstemmed notes only, except during the turnarounds

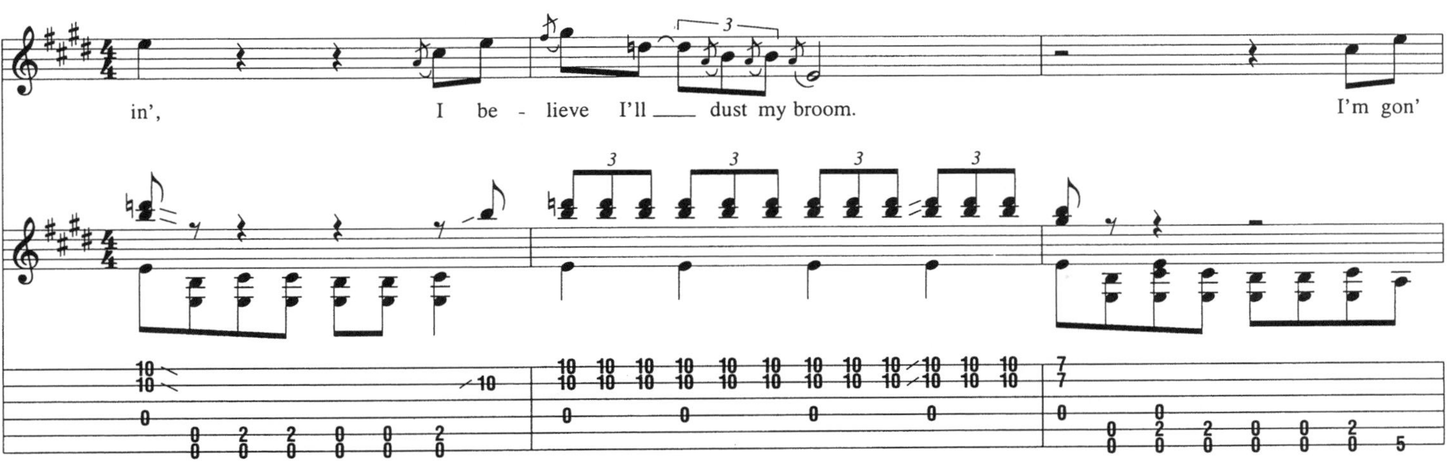

* Tunings were determined using the original 78s. To play along with the *Robert Johnson - The Complete Recordings* CD set, Capo I.

E7
B7
Girl-friend, the black man you been
lov-in',
A7
girl-friend, can get my room.
E/B
E7/D
A/C#
Am/C
* Sung behind the beat.
E/B
B9
Verse
E7
2. I'm gon' write a let-ter,
tel-e-phone
ev-'ry town I know.
A7
I'm gon' write a let-ter,

E7
tel - e - phone ev - 'ry town I know. _
B7
A7
If I can't find her in West Hel - 'na, _ she must be in East Mon - roe, I know. _
E
E7/D
A/C#
Am/C
E/B
B9
Verse
E7
3. I don't want no wom - an _ wants ev - 'ry
down - town _ man _ she meet. _ I don't

A7
want no wom-an wants ev-'ry down-town man she meet.
E7
B7
A7
She's a no good don - ey, they should-n't al-low her on the street.
E/B
E7/D
A/C#
Am/C
E/B
B7
Verse
E7
4. I be - lieve,
I be - lieve I'll go back home.

A7
I be - lieve, I
be - lieve I'll go back home.
E7
You can mis-treat
B7
me here, babe,
A7
but you can't when I go home.
E/B
E7/D
A/C#
Am/C
E/B
B9
Verse
E7
5. And I'm get-tin' up in the morn-in'.
I be -

A7
lieve I'll dust my broom. _ I'm get-tin' up in the morn-in'.
E7
I be-lieve I'll _ dust my _ broom. _ Girl-friend, the black
B7
A7
E7
A7
man you been lov - in', girl-friend, can get my room.
B7
Verse
E7
6. I'm gon' call up Chin - ey, see is my

A7
good girl o - ver there.
I'm gon' call up Chin-a,
see is
my good girl o - ver there.
E7
B7
'F I can't find her on Phil - li - pine's Is - land,
she
A7
E/B
E7/D
A/C#
Am/C
E/B
E7/B
must be in E - thi - o - pi - a some - where.

# Sweet Home Chicago

SA 2582 - 1

Words and Music by Robert Johnson

* Tunings were determined using the original 78s. To play along with the *Robert Johnson - The Complete Recordings* CD set, Capo III.

C♯7/G♯
(B7/F♯)
F♯
(E)
B
(A)
back to the land of Cal - i - for - nia, to my sweet home, Chi - ca - go?
F♯
(E)
F♯7
(E7)
F♯°7
(E°7)
Bm F♯7
(Am) (E7)
C♯7/G♯
(B7/F♯)
Verse
F♯7
(E7)
2. Oh,
B7
(A7)
F♯7
(E7)
ba - by don't you want to go?
Oh,
B7
(A7)
F♯7
(E7)
ba - by don't you want to go

C♯7/G♯
(B7/F♯)
F♯
(E)
B
(A)
back to the land of Cal - i - for - nia, to my sweet home, Chi - ca - go?
1/4 1/4 1/4 1/4 1/4
F♯
(E)
F♯7
(E7)
F♯°7
(E°7)
Bm F♯7
(Am) (E7)
C♯7/G♯
(B7/F♯)
Verse
F♯7
(E7)
3. Now, one and one is two.
Two and two is four.
I'm heav - y load - ed, ba - by. I'm
B7
(A7)
booked, I got - ta go. Cry - in' ba - by, hon - ey don't you want to

F#7
(E7)
C#7/G#
(B7/F#)
go
back to the land of Cal-i-for-nia, to my
F#
(E)
B
(A)
F#
(E)
F#7
(E7)
F#°7
(E°7)
Bm
(Am)
F#
(E)
C#7/G#
(B7/F#)
sweet home, Chi-ca-go?
4. Now,
Verse
F#7
(E7)
two and two is four.
Four and two is six.
You gon'
keep on monk-ey'n 'round here, freind-boy, gon' get your
busi-ness all in a trick.
But I'm cry-in'

B7
(A7)
F#7
(E7)
ba - by,
hon-ey don't you want to go
C#7/G#
(B7/F#)
F#
(E)
B
(A)
back to the land of Cal-i-for-nia, to my sweet home, Chi-ca-go?
F#
(E)
F#7
(E7)
F#°7
(E°7)
Bm F#
(Am) (E)
C#7
(B7)
Verse
F#7
(E7)
5. Now, six and two is eight.
Eight and two is ten.
Freind-boy, she trick you one time, she

B7
(A7)
sure gon' do it a - gain. But I'm cry'n' hey, hey,
F#7
(E7)
ba - by don't you want to go to the land
C#7/G#
(B7/F#)
F#
(E)
B
(A)
F#
(E)
F#7
(E7)
F#°7
(E°7)
Bm
(Am)
of Cal - i - for - nia, to my sweet home, Chi - ca - go?
F#
(E)
C#7/G#
(B7/F#)
Verse
F#7
(E7)
6. I'm go-in' to Cal - i - for - nia. From there to Des Moines, I 'way.

Some - bod - y will tell me that you need my help some - day. Cry'n'
B7
(A7)
hey, hey,
ba - by don't you want to go
F♯7
(E)
C♯7/G♯
(B7/F♯)
back to the land of Cal - i - for - nia, to my sweet home, Chi - ca - go?
F♯
(E)
B
(A)
1/4
F♯/C♯
(E/B)
F♯7/E
(E7/D)
B/D♯
(A/C♯)
Bm/D
(Am/C)
F♯/C♯
(E/B)
F♯7
(E7)

# Ramblin' on My Mind

**SA 2583 - 1**

**Words and Music by Robert Johnson**

* Open E Tuning, Down 1/2 Step; Capo II:

① = E♭ ④ = E♭

② = B♭ ⑤ = B♭

③ = G ⑥ = E♭

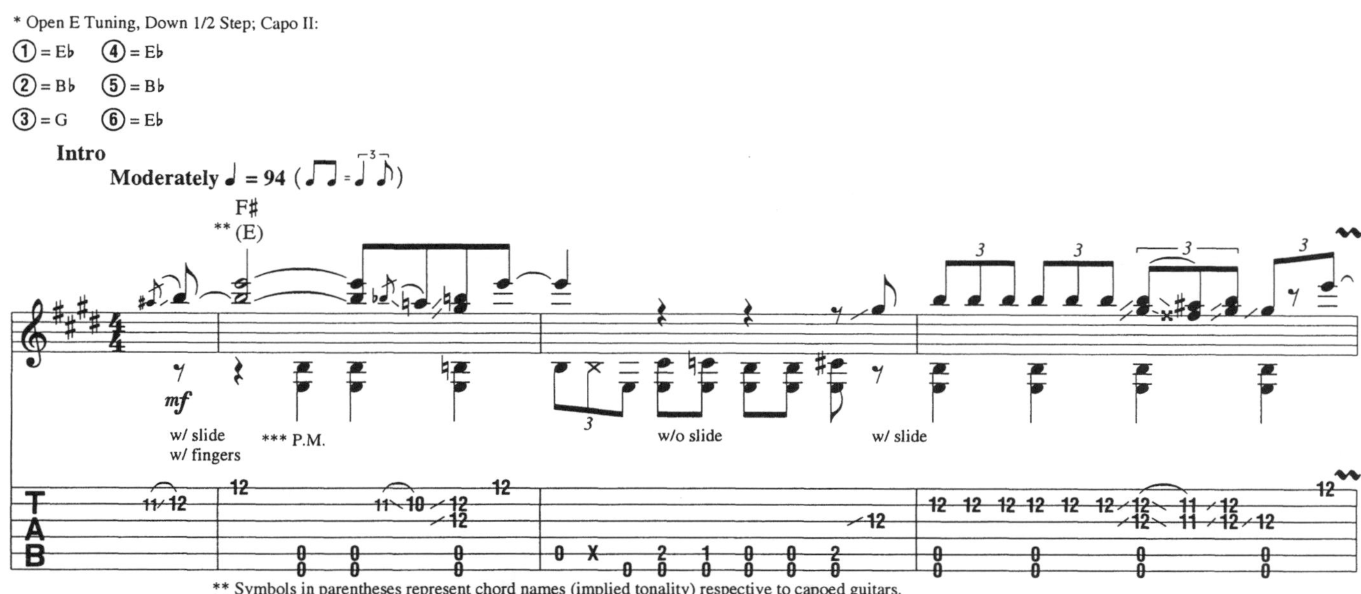


** Symbols in parentheses represent chord names (implied tonality) respective to capoed guitars. Symbols above reflect harmony implied by vocals. Capoed fret is "0" in TAB.

*** downstemmed notes only, except during the turnarounds

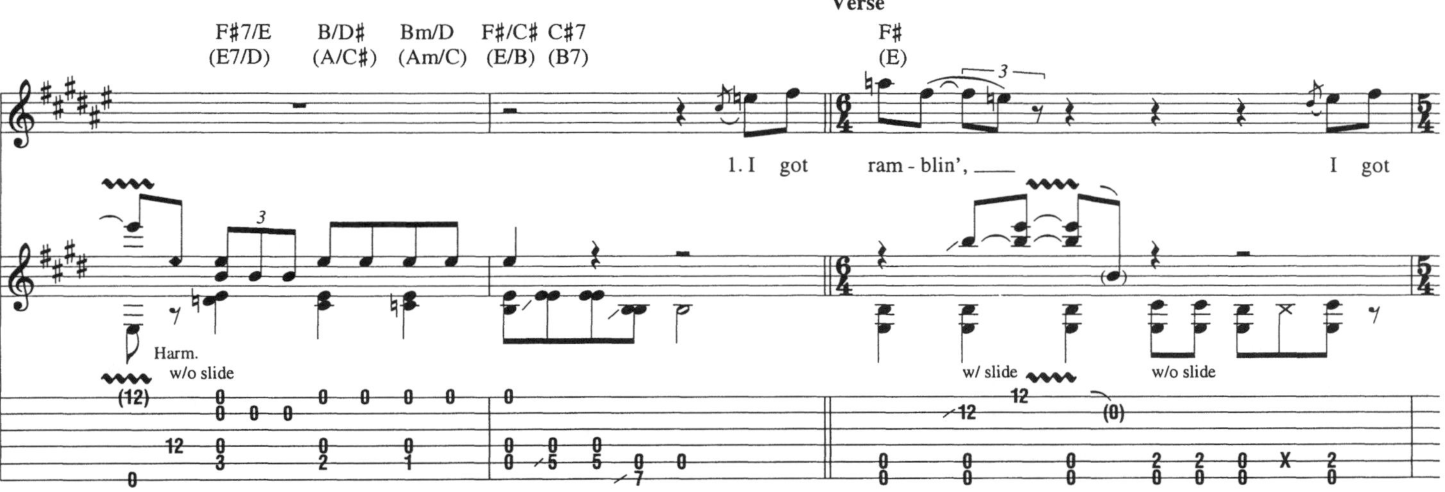

* Tunings were determined using the original 78s. To play along with the *Robert Johnson - The Complete Recordings* CD set, Capo III.

B
(A)
F♯
(E)
ram - blin',
I got ram-blin' all on my mind.
C♯
(B)
B
(A)
Hate to leave, my ba - by,
but you treats me so un - kind.
F♯7/E
(E7/D)
B/D♯
(A/C♯)
Bm/D
(Am/C)
F♯/C♯
(E/B)
C♯7
(B7)
Verse
F♯
(E)
2. I got mean things,
I got
w/ slide
mean things all on my mind.
Lit-tle girl, lit-tle
w/o slide
w/ slide
w/o slide

B
(A)
F♯
(E)
girl,
I got mean things all on my mind.
C♯
(B)
B
(A)
Hate to leave you here, babe,
but you treats me so un - kind.
F♯7/E
(E7/D)
B/D♯
(A/C♯)
Bm/D
(Am/C)
F♯/C♯
(E/B)
C♯7
(B7)
Verse
F♯
(E)
3. Run-nin' down to the sta - tion,
w/ slide
w/o slide
w/ slide
catch the first mail train I see.
Spoken: I think I hear it comin' now.
w/o slide
w/ slide
w/o slide
w/ slide

G#5 (F#5)
A5 (G5)
A#5 (G#5)
B (A)
Run-nin' down to the sta - tion,
w/o slide
F# (E)
catch that old first mail_train I see.
I got the blues
C# (B)
B (A)
F#7/E (E7/D)
B/D# (A/C#)
Bm/D (Am/C)
'bout Miss So-and-So, and the child got the blues a-bout me.
F#/C# (E/B)
C#7 (B7)
Verse
F# (E)
4. And I'm leav-in' this morn-in' with my arm' fold' up and cry'n'.
w/ slide
w/o slide
w/ slide
w/o slide
w/ slide

G#5 A5 A#5 F#
(F#5)(G5) (G#5)(E)
w/o slide
w/ slide
B
(A)
And I'm leav - in' this morn - in' with my arm' fold'_upped and cry'n'.
w/o slide
F#
(E)
C#
(B)
I hate to leave my ba - by, but
B
(A)
F#/C# F#7 B/D# Bm/D F#/C# C#7
(E/B) (E7) (A/C#) (Am/C) (E/B) (B7)
she treats me so un - kind.
5. I got mean
w/ slide

Verse
F♯
(E)
— things, I've got mean – things – on my mind. —
w/o slide
B
(A)
I got mean things, — I
w/ slide
w/o slide
got mean things – all on my mind. ——
F♯
(E)
I got to
C♯
(B)
B
(A)
leave me ba - by. – Well, she treats me – so — un - kind. ——
F♯7
(E7)
B/D♯
(A/C♯)
Bm/D
(Am/C)
F♯/C♯
(E/B)
C♯7
(B7)
F♯
(E)
w/ slide

# When You Got a Good Friend

SA 2584 - 1

Words and Music by Robert Johnson

* Tune Down 1/2 Step; Capo II:

① = Eb ④ = Db

② = Bb ⑤ = Ab

③ = Gb ⑥ = Eb

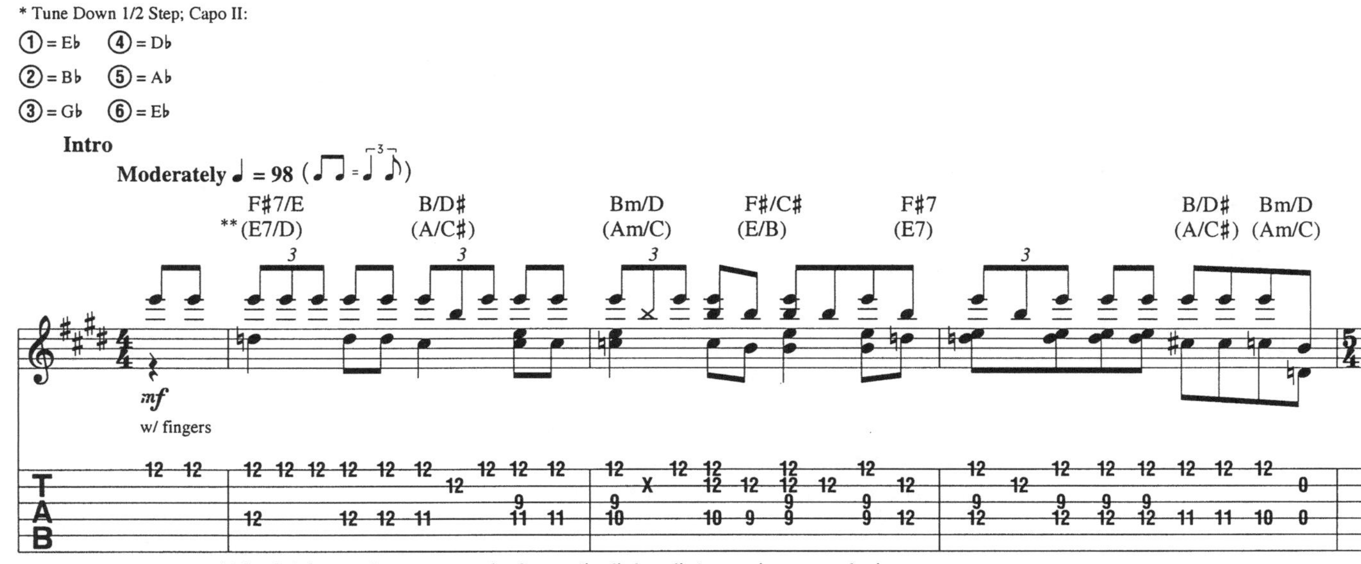


** Symbols in parentheses represent chord names (implied tonality) respective to capoed guitar. Symbols above reflect harmony implied by vocals. Capoed fret is "0" in TAB.

*** downstemmed notes only, except during the turnarounds

* Tunings were determined using the original 78s. To play along with the *Robert Johnson - The Complete Recordings* CD set, Capo III.

F♯7
(E7)
that will stay right by your side,
C♯/G♯
(B/F♯)
F♯
(E)
B
(A)
give her all your spare time,
love and treat her
1/4 1/4 1/4 1/4 1/4
F♯
(E)
F♯7
(E7)
F♯°7
(E°7)
Bm
(Am)
F♯
(E)
C♯7/G♯
(B7/F♯)
Verse
F♯7
(E7)
right.
2. I mis-treat-ed my ba-by
B7
(A7)
F♯7
(E7)
and I can't see no rea-son why.
I

* ③ is bumped with tip of L.H. middle finger, not fretted.

F#7
(E7)
B7
(A7)
Mmm,
would she sym-pa-thize with me?
She's a brown-
skin wom-an,
just as sweet as a girl friend can be.
C#7/G#
(B7/F#)
F#
(E)
B
(A)
F#7
F#°7
(E°7)
Bm
(Am)
F#/C#
(E/B)
Verse
4. Mmm,

B7
(A7)
F#7
(E7)
babe, I may be right ay wrong.
Ba-by, it's yo'y
B7
(A7)
F#7
(E7)
o - pin - ion,
oh I may be right ay wrong.
C#7/G#
(B7/F#)
F#
(E)
B
(A)
Watch your close friend, ba - by,
then your en-e'ies can't do you no harm.
F#
(E)
F#7
(E7)
F#°7
(E°7)
Bm
(Am)
F#
(E)
C#7/G#
(B7/F#)
Verse
F#7
(E7)
5. When you got a good friend

B7
(A7)
F#7
(E7)
that will stay right by your side,
when you
got a good friend
that will stay right by your side,
C#7/G#
(B7/F#)
F#
(E)
B
(A)
give her all of your spare time - aah,
love and treat her right.
* ③ is bumped with tip of L.H. middle finger, not fretted.
F#/C#
(E/B)
F#7/E
(E7/D)
B/D#
(A/C#)
Bm/D
(Am/C)

# Come on in My Kitchen

**SA 2585 - 1**

**Words and Music by Robert Johnson**

* Open A Tuning, Down 1/2 Step; Capo II:

① = E♭ ④ = E♭
② = C ⑤ = A♭
③ = A♭ ⑥ = E♭

**Intro**

**Moderately Slow** ♩ = 81

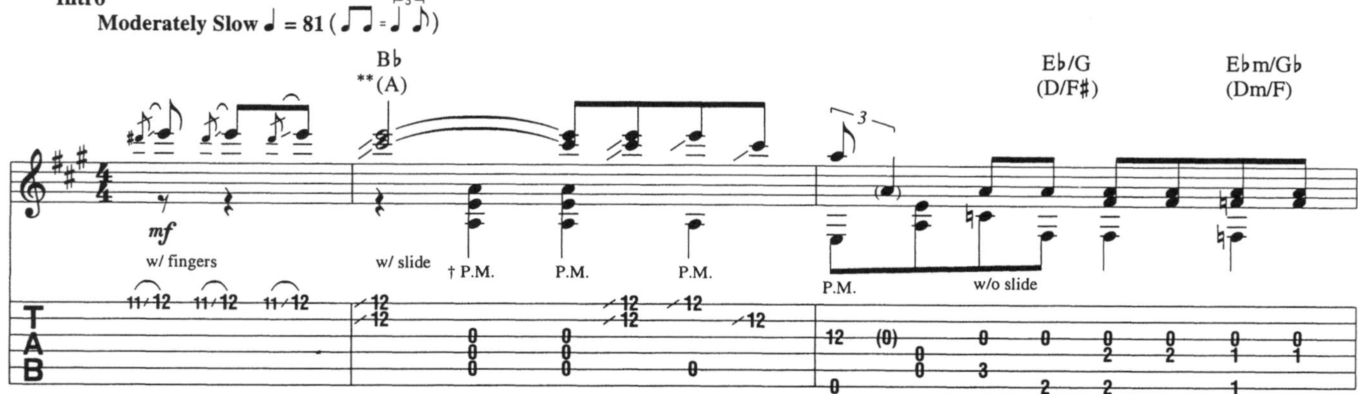


** Symbols in parentheses represent chord names (implied tonality) respective to capoed guitar. Symbols above reflect harmony implied by vocals. Capoed fret is "0" in TAB.
† downstemmed notes only

*** downstemmed notes only.

* Tunings were determined using the original 78s.

en. Babe, it's go-in' to be rain - in' out - doors.
Verse
B♭
(A)
2. Ah, the wom-an I love took from my best
w/o slide w/ slide w/o slide w/ slide
friend. Some jok - er got luck - y, stole her back a - gain.
You bet-ter come on in my kitch - en. Ba - by, it's
w/o slide w/ slide

go - in' to be rain - in' out - doors.
Verse
B♭
(A)
3. Oh - ah, she's gone. I know she won't come
w/o slide
w/ slide
back. I've tak - en the last nick - el out of her na - tion
* even
* Played as even eighth notes.
sack. You bet - ter come on in my kitch - en. Babe, it's
w/o slide
w/ slide
w/o slide

Bridge
B♭
(A)
go-in' to be rain - in' out - doors.
Spoken: Oh, can't you hear
w/ slide
w/o slide
w/ slide
the wind howl 'n' all?
Oh-y' can't you hear that wind would howl?
p
* Slide positioned halfway between 14th & 15th frets.
You bet-ter come on in my kitch - en. Ba - by, it's
w/o slide
go-in' to be rain - in' out - doors.
w/ slide
w/o slide
w/ slide
w/o slide

Verse
B♭
(A)
4. When a wom-an gets in trou - ble, ev - 'ry-bod - y throws her down.
w/ slide
F7
(E7)
B♭
(A)
Look-in' for her good friend, none can be found. You bet-ter come
w/o slide
w/ slide
on in my kitch - en. Ba - by, it's gon' to be rain - in' out - doors.
5. Win-ter time's com -
w/o slide
w/ slide
w/o slide
w/ slide
w/o slide
* w/ slide
* upstemmed note only

Verse
B♭
(A)
in', hit's gon' be slow. You can't make the win - ter,
babe, that's dry long so. You bet - ter come
on in my kitch - en 'cause it's
gon' to be rain - in' out - doors.
w/o slide
w/ slide
5:4

# Terraplane Blues

SA 2586 - 1

Words and Music by Robert Johnson

* Open A Tuning, Down 1/2 Step; Capo II:
① = E♭ ④ = E♭
② = C ⑤ = A♭
③ = A♭ ⑥ = E♭

**Intro**

**Moderately** ♩ = 101

B **(A) B7 (A7)

*mf*

w/ slide
w/ fingers

w/o slide

1. And I

** Symbols in parentheses represent chord names (implied tonality) respective to capoed guitar. Symbols above reflect harmony implied by vocals. Capoed fret is "0" in TAB.

**Verse**

B7 (A7)

feel so lone - some, you hear me when I moan.

E7 (D7)

When I feel so lone - some, you hear me when I moan.

1/4 1/4 1/4

B7 (A7) F♯7♯9 (E7♯9) E7 (D7)

Who been driv-in' my Ter-ra-plane for

w/ slide

* Tunings were determined using the original 78s.

B7
(A7)
you since I been gone?
2. I'd
w/o slide

Verse
B7
(A7)
said I flash your lights, ma - ma.
Your horn won't e - ven blow. Spoken: Some -

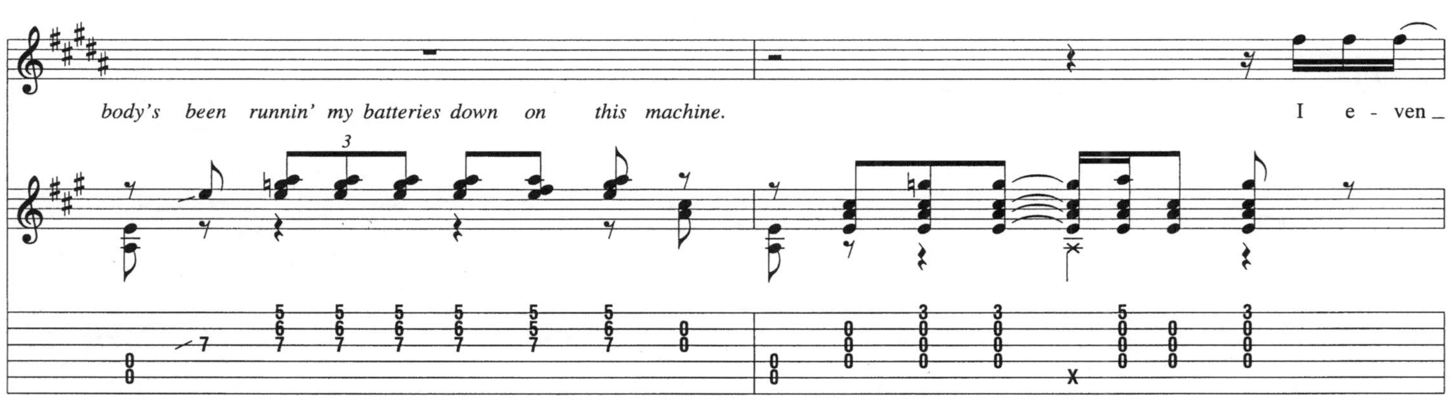
body's been runnin' my batteries down on this machine.
I e - ven

E7
(D7)
flash my lights, ma - ma.
This horn won't e - ven blow.
1/4

B7
(A7)
F#7#9
(E7#9)
E7
(D7)
Got a short in this con-nec-tion. Hoo-
w/ slide
well, babe, it's way down_ be - low. ______
3. I'm
w/o slide
Verse
'on' h'ist your hood, ma - ma. __
I'm bound to check_ your oil. ______
I'm gon' h'ist your hood, ma - ma. __
1/4
* Tap finger on guitar body.

B7
(A7)
I'm bound to check your oil.
I got a
1/4
* Tap finger on guitar body
F#7#9
(E7#9)
E7
(D7)
wom-an that I'm lov - in' way down in Ar-kan - sas.
w/ slide
w/o slide
Bridge
B7
(A7)
Now, you know the coils ain't e - ven buz - zin'. Lit - tle
gen - er - a - tor won't get the spark. Mot-or's in a bad con-di - tion. You got - ta have

E7
(D7)
these bat-t'ries charged. _ But I'm cry'n'_ please, _
plea - hease don't do me wrong. _
1/4
1/4
B7
(A7)
F#7#9
(E7#9)
E7
(D7)
Who been driv - in' my Ter-ra-plane now for
w/ slide
w/o slide
w/ slide
B7
(A7)
you - hoo since I _____ been gone? ___
4. Mis-ter
w/o slide
Verse
B7
(A7)
High - way - man, ___
plea - hease don't block the road. _______

E7
(D7)
Puh hee ___ hee, ___ plea - hease ___ don't block the road. ___
1/4
1/4
B7
(A7)
F#7#9
(E7#9)
E7
(D7)
'Cause she re'ist'r-in' a cold ___ one hun- dred and I'm
w/ slide
booked and I got to go. ___
B7
(A7)
w/o slide
Verse
B7
(A7)
5. Mmm, ___ mmm. ___ Mmm, ___ mmm. ___

E7
(D7)
You,
B7
(A7)
you hear me weep_ and moan.
w/ slide
w/o slide
Who been
F#7#9
(E7#9)
E7
(D7)
B7
(A7)
driv - in' my Ter-ra-plane now for
you - hoo since I been gone?
w/ slide
w/o slide
Verse
B7
(A7)
6. I'm 'on' get deep down in this con-nec - tion,

keep on tang-lin' with your wires.
I 'on'
E7
(D7)
get deep down in this con-nec - tion,
hoo - well, keep on tang-lin' with these wires.
1/4
1/4
B7
(A7)
F#7#9
(E7#9)
E7
(D7)
And when I mash down on your lit-tle start - er, then your
w/ slide
spark plug will give me fire.
w/o slide
B/F#
(A/E)
B7
(A7)
E/G#
(D/F#)
Em/G
(Dm/F)
B/F#
(A/E)
B
(A)
w/ slide

# Phonograph Blues

SA 2587 - 1

Words and Music by Robert Johnson

* Tune Down 1/2 Step; Capo II:

① = E♭ ④ = D♭

② = B♭ ⑤ = A♭

③ = G♭ ⑥ = E♭

**Intro**

**Moderately** ♩ = 93

B (A) — B°7 (A°7) — F#9 (E9) — B (A) — B7/A (A7/G) — E/G# (D/F#) — Em/G (Dm/F)

*mf*

w/ fingers

** Symbols in parentheses represent chord names (implied tonality) respective to capoed guitar. Symbols above reflect harmony implied by vocals. Capoed fret is "0" in TAB.

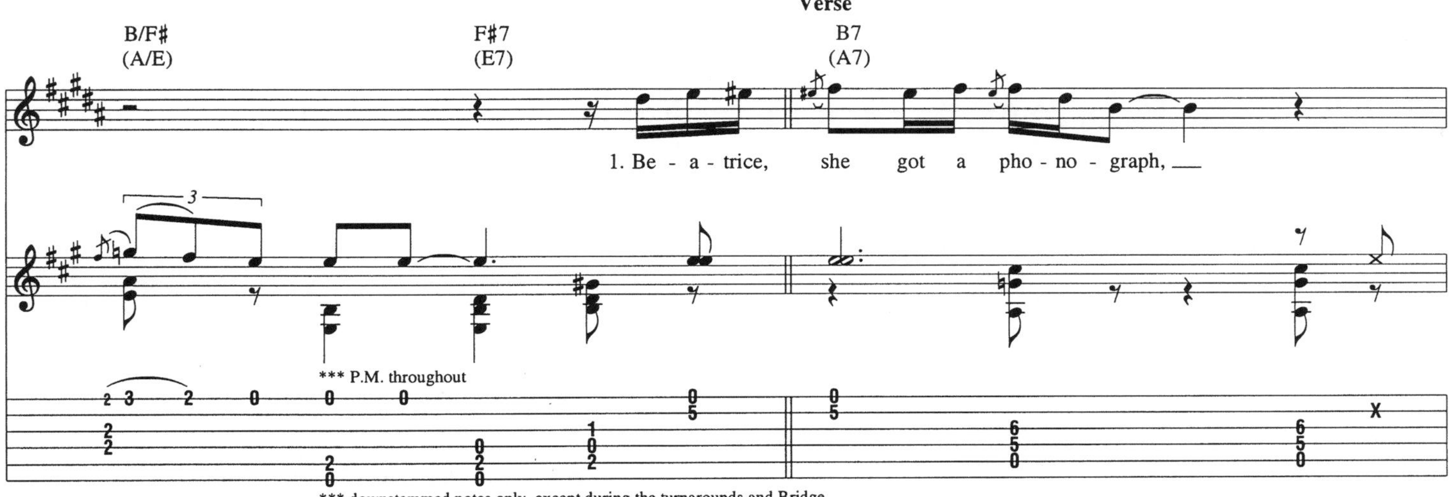

* Tunings were determined using the original 78s. To play along with the *Robert Johnson - The Complete Recordings* CD set, Capo III.

E7/G#
(D7/F#)
she got a pho - no - graph,
but it won't say a lone - some word.
* Sung behind the beat.
B7
(A7)
B°7
(A°7)
B7
(A7)
F#7
(E7)
What e - vil have I done?
What
E7/G#
(D7/F#)
B
(A)
B7/A
(A7/G)
E/G#
(D/F#)
Em/G
(Dm/F)
B/F#
(A/E)
F#7
(E7)
e - vil has the poor girl heard?
2. Be-a-trice, I
Verse
B7
(A7)
B°7
(A°7)
love my pho - no - graph,
but you have broke my wind - in' chain.

B7 (A7)
B°7 (A°7)
B7 (A7)
E7/F♯ (D7/F♯)
Be-a-trice, I love my pho-no-gra'-ooo.
B7 (A7)
B°7 (A°7)
B7 (A7)
Hon-ey, I broke my wind-in' chain.
And you've
F♯7 (E7)
E7/G♯ (D7/F♯)
B (A)
B7/A (A7G)
E/G♯ (D/F♯)
Em/G (Dm/F)
tak-in' my lov-in' and give it to your oth-er man.
B/F♯ (A/E)
F♯7 (E7)
Bridge
B7 (A7)
B°7 (A°7)
Now, we played it on the so-fa, now. We played it 'side the wall. My

B7 (A7)
B°7 (A°7)
B7 (A7)
B°7 (A°7)
B7 (A7)
need - les have got rust - y, ba - by, they will not play at all. We played it on the
E7/G♯ (D7/F♯)
B7 (A7)
B°7 (A°7)
so - fa, and we played it 'side the wall.
* P.M.
* Resume P.M. on downstem notes.
B7 (A7)
F♯7 (E7)
E7/G♯ (D7/F♯)
But my need-les have got rust - y and it will not play at all.
B/F♯ (A/E)
B7/A (A7/G)
E/G♯ (D/F♯)
Em/G (Dm/F)
B/F♯ (A/E)
F♯7 (E7)
Verse
B7 (A7)
3. Be-a-trice, I go cra - zy.

B°7
(A°7)
B7
(A7)
B°7
(A°7)
B7
(A7)
Ba-by, I will lose my mind.
And
E7/G#
(D7/F#)
I go cra' - eee,
hon-ey, I will lose my mind.
B7
(A7)
B°7
(A°7)
B7
(A7)
Why-n't you bring your clothes back home
F#7
(E7)
E7/G#
(D7/F#)
and try me one more time.
B
(A)
B7/A
(A7/G)
E/G#
(D/F#)
Em/G
(Dm/F)
B/F#
(A/E)
F#7
(E7)
Verse
B7
(A7)
4. She got a pho - no - graph

B°7
(A°7)
B7
(A7)
and it won't say a lone-some word.
She
E7/G♯
(D7/F♯)
got a pho - no - graph,
ooo,
won't say a lone - some word.
B7
(A7)
B°7
(A°7)
B7
(A7)
F♯7
(E7)
What e - vil have I done,
E7/G♯
(D7/F♯)
B
(A)
B7/A
(A7/G)
E/G♯
(D/F♯)
Em/G
(Dm/F)
F♯7/C♯
(E7/B)
B7
(A7)
or what e - vil have the poor girl heard?

# Phonograph Blues

**SA 2587 - 2**

**Words and Music by Robert Johnson**

E7
won't say a lone-some word.
What e-vil
B7
A7
E/B
E7/D
A/C#
Am/C
have I done?
What e-vil have the poor girl heard?
E/B
B7
Verse
E7
2. Be-a-trice, I love my pho-no-graph, but you broke my wind-in' chain.
A7
Be-a-trice, I love my pho-no-graph, but you

E7
have broke my wind-in' chain.
And you tak-
B7
A7
E/B
E7/D
A/C♯
Am/C
en my lov-in' and you gave it to yo' oth - er man.
E/B
B7
Verse
E7
3. And we played it on the so - fa, and we played it 'side the wall.
A7
And we played it on the so - fa, and we

E7
played it 'side the wall.
But boys, my
B7
A7
E/B
E7/D
A/C♯
Am/C
need-les have got rust - y
and it will not play a - t'all.
Verse
E/B
B7
E7
4. Mmm, Beez-a - trice,
I love my pho-no - graph,
mmm,
babe, and I'm
A7
bound to lose my mind.
Be - a-trice, I love my pho - no-graph,
and I'm

E7
___ 'bout to lose my mind.
Why'n't you bring
B7
A7
your clothes _ back home ___ ba - by and try me one more __ time. ___
E/B
E7/D
A/C#
Am/C
E/B
B7
Verse
E7
5. Now my pho - no - graph, _ mmm, _ babe, _ it
won't say a lone - some word. __

A7
My lit-tle pho - no - graph, and it won't say a lone-some word.
E7
B7
What e - vil have I done? What
A7
E
E7/D
A/C#
Am/C
E/B
B7
e - vil has the poor girl heard?
6. Now Be -
Verse
E7
a - trice, won't you bring your clothes back home?

A7
Now Be - a - trice, won't you
bring your clothes back home?
E7
B7
I wan - na wind your lit - tle pho - no - graph _ just to ___
A7
___ hear your lit - tle mo - tor moan.
E/B
E7/D
A/C♯
Am/C
E/B
E7
1/4

# 32-20 Blues

* Tune Down 1/2 Step, Capo I:
① = E♭ ④ = D♭
② = B♭ ⑤ = A♭
③ = G♭ ⑥ = E♭

SA 2616 - 2

Words and Music by Robert Johnson

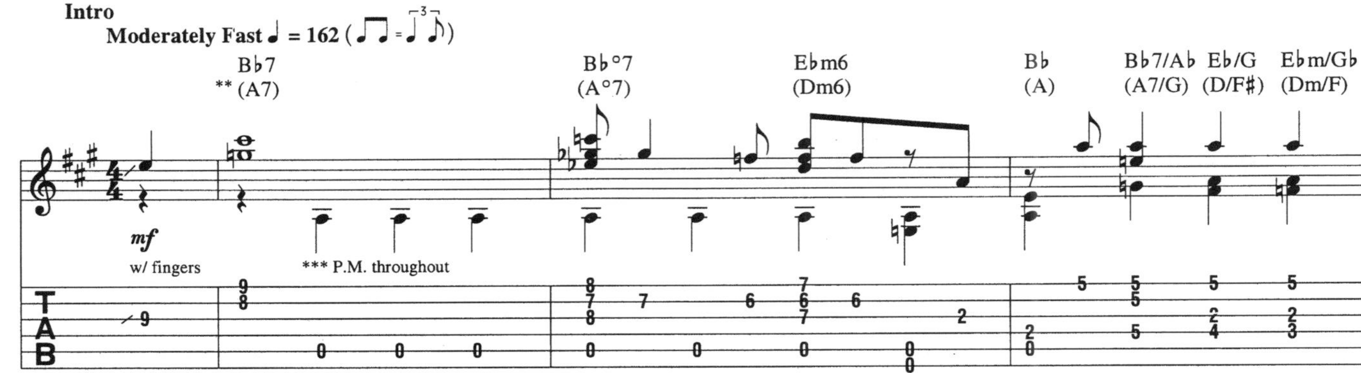


** Symbols in parentheses represent chord names (implied tonality) respective to capoed guitar. Symbols above reflect harmony implied by vocals. Capoed fret is "0" in TAB.

*** downstemmed notes only

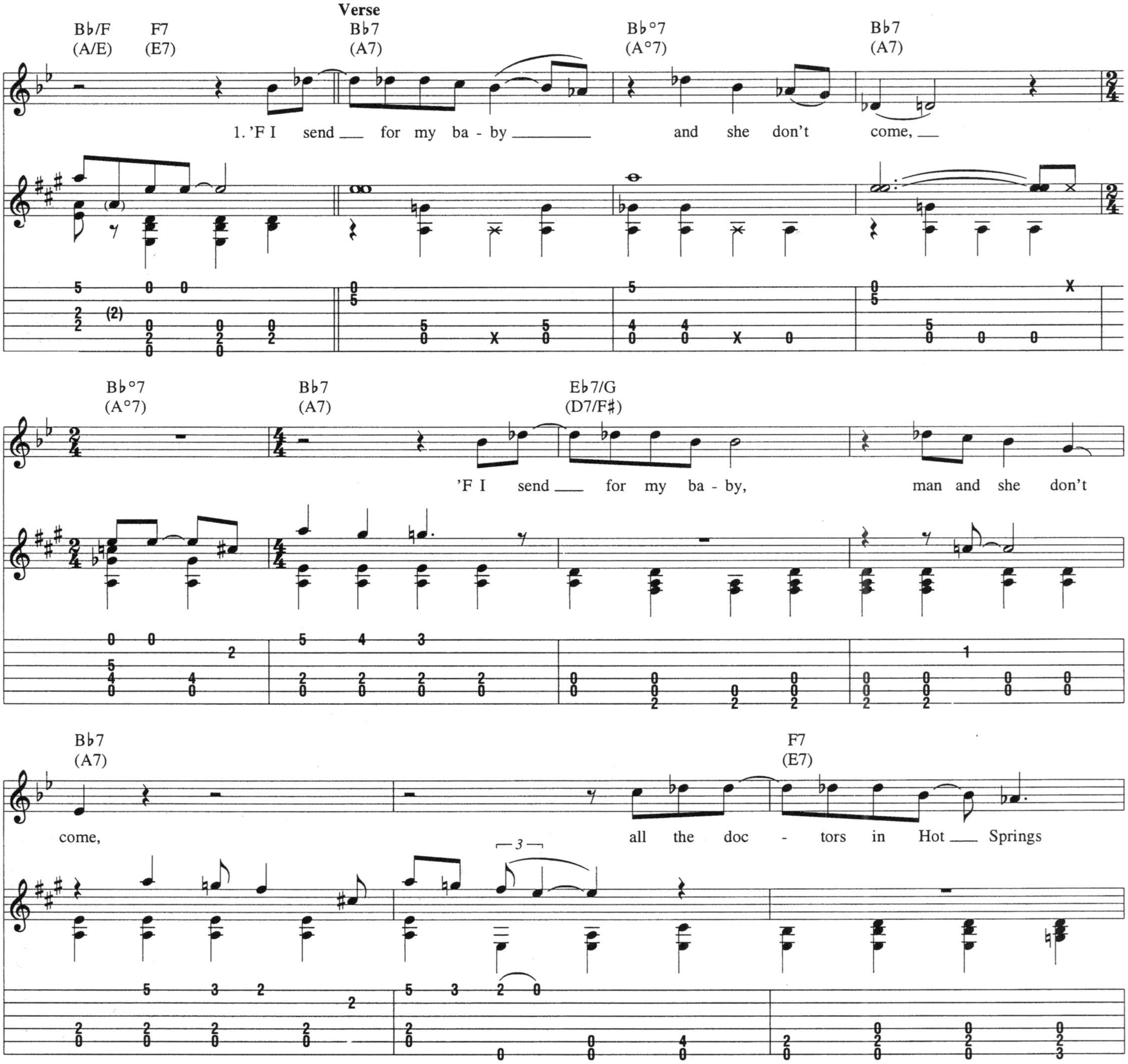

B♭/F (A/E) F7 (E7)

**Verse**

B♭7 (A7) B♭°7 (A°7) B♭7 (A7)

1. 'F I send __ for my ba - by __ and she don't come, __

B♭°7 (A°7) B♭7 (A7) E♭7/G (D7/F♯)

'F I send __ for my ba - by, man and she don't

B♭7 (A7) F7 (E7)

come, all the doc - tors in Hot __ Springs

* Tunings were determined using the original 78s.

Verse
Eb7/G (D7/F#)
Bb (A)
Bb7/Ab (A7/G)
Eb/G (D/F#)
Ebm/Gb (Dm/F)
F7 (E7)
Bb7 (A7)
sure can't help her none.
2. And if she gets un-rul-y,
Bb°7 (A°7)
A7
thinks she don't wan' do,
if she gets un-rul-y and
thinks she don't wan' do,
take my thir-ty two twen-ty now and
Bb/F (A/E)
cut her half in two.
3. She got a thir-ty eight spe-cial but I

Bb°7
(A°7)
Bb7
(A7)
Eb/G
(D7/F#)
b'lieve it's most too light.
She got a thir - ty eight spe - cial but I
Bb7
(A7)
F7
(E7)
Bb7
(A7)
b'lieve it's most too light.
I got a
F7
(E7)
Eb7/G
(D7/F#)
Bb
(A)
Bb7
(A7)
Eb/G
(D/F#)
Ebm/Gb
(Dm/F)
Bb/F
(A/E)
F7
(E7)
thir - ty two twen - ty, got to make the camps al - right.
4. If I
Verse
Bb7
(A7)
Bb°7
(A°7)
Bb7
(A7)
send for my ba - by, man, and she don't come,
if I send

Eb7/G
(D7/F#)
Bb7
(A7)
for my ba - by, man and she don't come, all the doc -
F7
(E7)
Eb7/G
(D7/F#)
Bb
(A)
Bb7/Ab Eb/G Ebm/Gb Bb/F F7
(A7/G)(D/F#)(Dm/F) (A/E) (E7)
- tors in Hot Springs sure can't help her none.
5. I'm gon - na
Verse
Bb7
(A7)
Bb°7
(A°7)
Bb7
(A7)
shoot my pis - tol, gon - na shoot my Gat - ling gun.
I'm 'on - na
Eb7/G
(D7/F#)
Bb7
(A7)
shoot my pis - tol, got - ta shoot my Gat - ling gun.
You made

F7
(E7)
Eb7/G
(D7/F#)
Bb
(A)
Bb7/Ab Eb/G Ebm/Gb Bb F7
(A7/G)(D/F#)(Dm/F) (A) (E7)
me love you, now your man have come.
Verse
Bb
(A)
Bbm7
(Am7)
Bb
(A)
Bb7
(A7)
6. Ah - oh, ba - by where you stay last night?
Eb/G
(D/F#)
Bb7
(A7)
Ah - ah, ba - by where you stayed last night? You got the
* Sung behind the beat.
F7
(E7)
Eb/G
(D/F#)
Bb
(A)
Bb7/Ab Eb/G Ebm/Gb Bb/F F7
(A7/G)(D/F#)(Dm/F) (A/E) (E7)
hair all tan - gled and you ain't talk - in' right. 7. Got a thir -

Verse
B♭7
(A7)
B♭°7
(A°7)
B♭7
(A7)
- ty eight spe - cial, _ boys, hit do ver - y well. _ A thir -
E♭7/G
(D7/F♯)
B♭7
(A7)
- ty eight spe - cial, boys, it do ver - y well. ___ I got a
F7
(E7)
E♭7/G
(D7/F♯)
B♭
(A)
B♭7/A♭ E♭/G E♭m/G♭ B♭/F F7
(A7/G)(D/F♯)(Dm/F) (A/E) (E7)
thir - ty two twen - ty, now, and it's a burn - in'.... _ 8. If I send _
Verse
B♭7
(A7)
B♭°7
(A°7)
B♭7
(A7)
____ for my ba - by, man, and she _ don't come, if I

Eb7/G
(D7/F#)
Bb7
(A7)
send for my ba - by, man, and she don't come, all the doc -
F7
(E7)
Eb7/G
(D7/F#)
Bb Bb7 Eb/G Ebm/Gb Bb/F F7
(A) (A7) (D/F#) (Dm/F) (A/E) (E7)
- tors in Wis-con-sin sure can't help her none. 9. Hey
Verse
Bb7
(A7)
Bb°7
(A°7)
Bb7
(A7)
hey, ba - by, where you stay last night? Hey,
Eb7/G
(D7/F#)
Bb7
(A7)
hey, babe, where you stayed last night? You did -

F7
(E7)
Eb7/G
(D7/F#)
Bb
(A)
Bb/Ab Eb/G Ebm/Gb Bb/F F7
(A7/G) (D/F#) (Dm/F) (A/E) (E7)
n't come home _ un - til the sun was shin - in' bright. _
Verse
Bb
(A)
A
(G#)
Bb
(A)
Bb7
(A7)
10. Ah, boys, I just can't take my rest. ___ Ah, _
Eb7/G
(D7/F#)
Bb7
(A7)
boys, I just can't take _ my rest ___ with this
F7
(E7)
Eb7/G
(D7/F#)
Bb Bb7/Ab Eb/G Ebm/Gb F7
(A) (A7/G) (D/F#) (Dm/F) (E7)
Bb7
(A7)
thir - ty two twen - ty lay - in' up and down _ my breast. _

*Tune Down 1/2 Step; Capo I:

(1) = Eb (4) = Db
(2) = Bb (5) = Ab
(3) = Gb (6) = Eb

SA 2627 - 1

Words and Music by Robert Johnson

**Intro**

Moderately Fast ♩ = 109

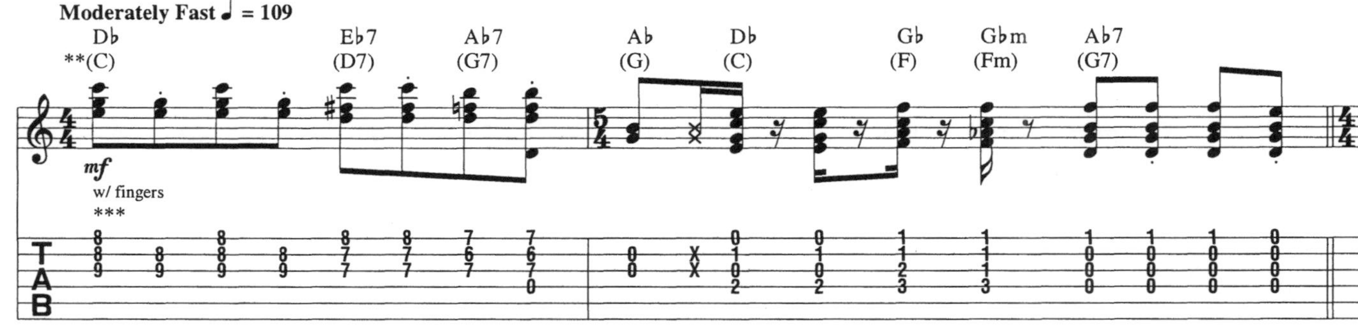


** Symbols in parentheses represent chord names respective to capoed guitar. Symbols above reflect harmony implied by vocals. Capoed fret is "0" in TAB.

*** chords strummed w/ thumb throughout

**Verse**

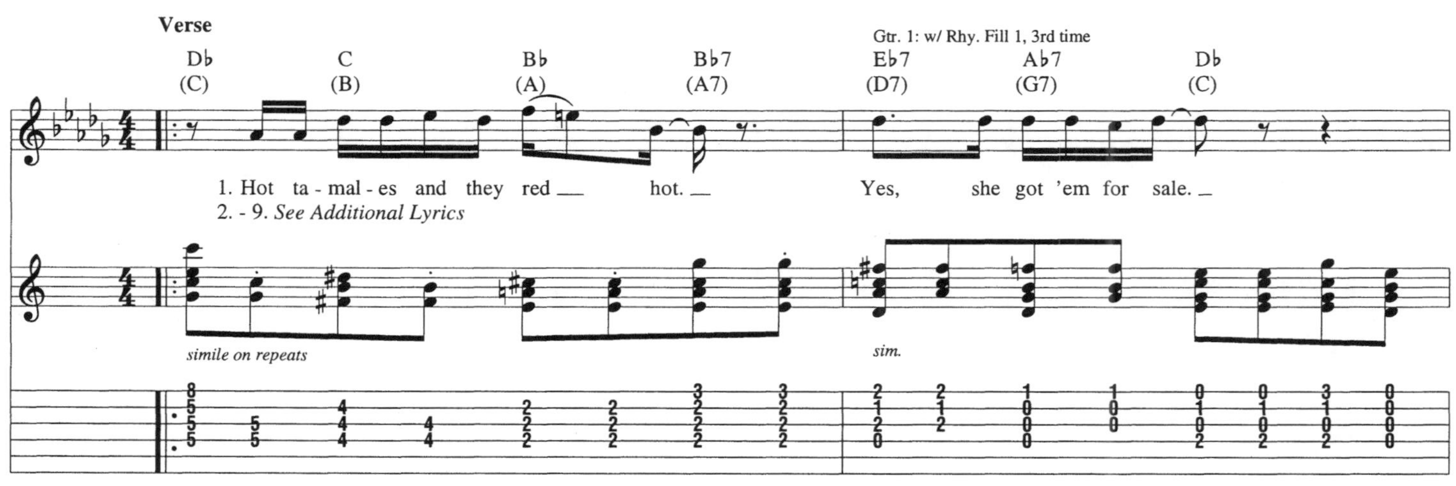


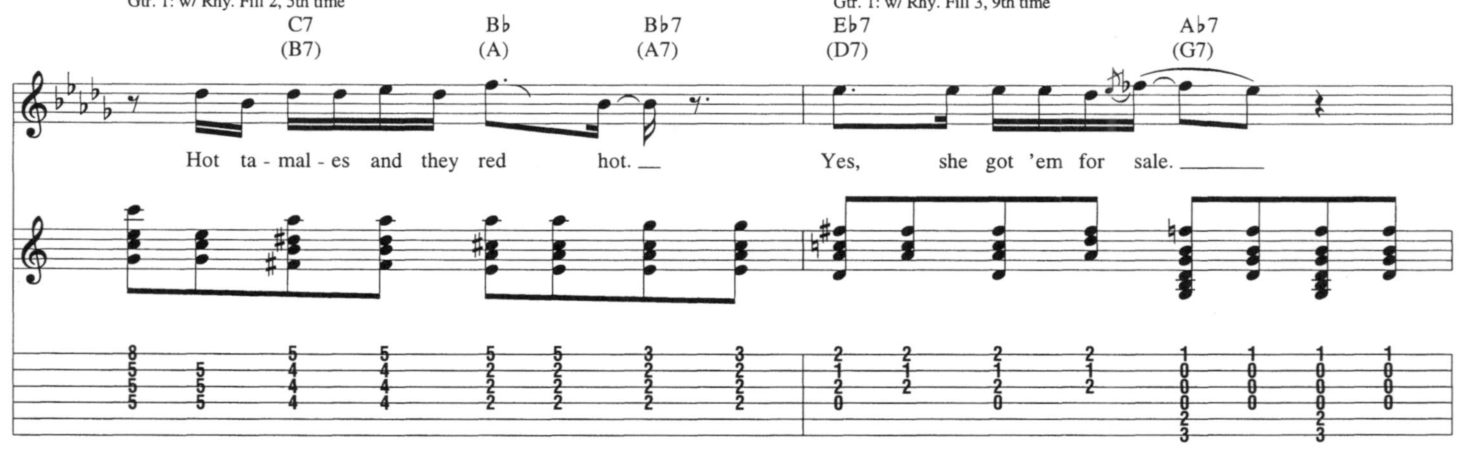


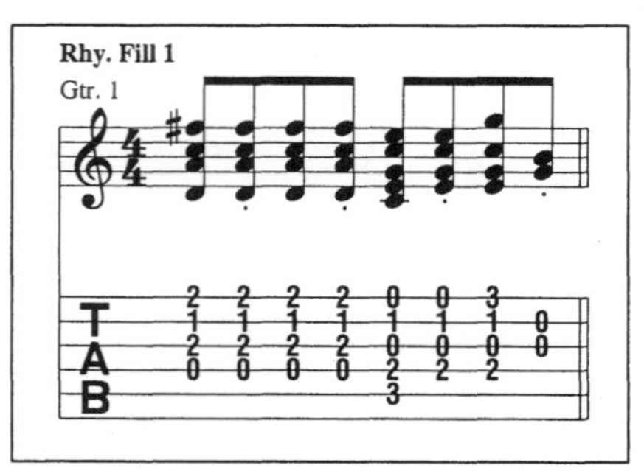


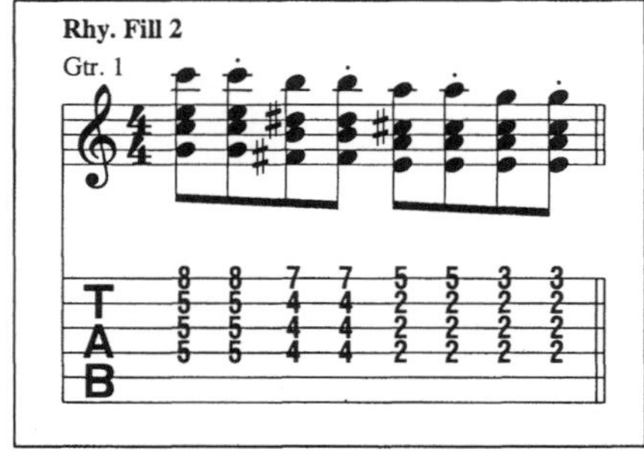


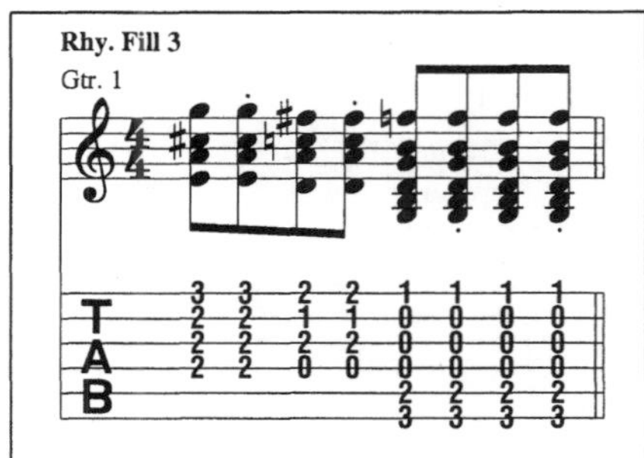


* Tunings were determined using the original 78s.

*Additional Lyrics*

2. Hot tamales and they red hot.
   Yes, she got 'em for sale.
   Hot tamales and they red hot.
   Yes, she got 'em for sale.
   She got two for a nickel, got four for a dime.
   Would sell you more, but they ain't none of mine.
   Hot tamales and they red hot.
   Yes, she got 'em for sale.
   I mean, yes she got 'em for sale, yes, yeah.

3. Hot tamales and they red hot.
   Yes, she got 'em for sale.
   Hot tamales and they red hot.
   Yes, she got 'em for sale.
   I got a letter from a girl in the room.
   How, she got somethin' good she got to bring home soon, now.
   It's hot tamales and they red hot.
   Yes, she got 'em for sale.
   I mean, yes, she got 'em for sale, yeah.

4. Hot tamales and they red hot.
Yes, she got 'em for sale.
Hot tamales and they red hot.
Yes, she got 'em for sale. *They're too hot, boy!*
The billy goat back' in a bumble bee nest.
Ever since that, he can't take his rest, yeah.
Hot tamales and they red hot.
Yeah, you got 'em for sale.
I mean, yes, she got 'em for sale.

5. Hot tamales and they red hot.
Yes, she got 'em for sale.
*Man, don't mess around 'em hot tamales, now*
*'Cause they too black bad.*
*If you mess around 'em hot tamales,*
*I'm 'onna upset your backbone, put your kidneys to sleep.*
*I'll due to break 'way your livin' and dare your heart to beat 'bout my*
Hot tamales 'cause they red hot.
Yes, they got 'em for sale.
I mean, yes, she got 'em for sale, yeah.

6. Hot tamales and they red hot.
Yes, she got 'em for sale.
Hot tamales and they red hot.
Yes, she got 'em for sale.
You know grandma laughs, and now grandpa too.
Well, I wonder what in the world we chillun gon' do, now.
Hot tamales and they red hot.
Yes, she got' 'em for sale.
I mean, yes, she got 'em for sale.

7. Hot tamales and they red hot.
Yes, she got 'em for sale.
Hot tamales and they red hot.
Yes, she got 'em for sale.
Me and my babe bought a V-8 Ford.
Well, we wind that thing all on the runnin' board, yes.
Hot tamales and they red hot.
Yes, she got 'em for sale.
I mean, yes she got 'em for sale, yeah.

8. Hot tamales and they red hot.
Yes, she got 'em, for sale. *They're too hot, boy!*
Hot tamales and they red hot.
Yes, now, she got 'em for sale.
You know the monkey, now the baboon playin' in the grass.
Well, the monkey stuck his finger in that old "Good Gulf Gas," now.
Hot tamales and they red hot.
Yes, she got 'em for sale.
I mean, yes, she got 'em for sale, yeah.

9. Hot tamales and they red hot.
Yes, she got 'em for sale.
Hot tamales and they red hot.
Yes, she got 'em for sale.
I got a girl, say she long and tall.
Now, she sleeps in the kitchen with her feets in the hall, yes.
Hot tamales and they red hot.
Yes, now, she got 'em for sale.
I mean, yes, she got 'em for sale, yeah.

# Dead Shrimp Blues

SA 2628 - 2

Words and Music by Robert Johnson

* Tunings were determined using the original 78s. To play along with the *Robert Johnson - The Complete Recordings* CD set, Capo III.

E7/G#
(D7/F#)
B7
(A7)
B°7
(A°7)
this morn-in', ooh, all my shrimps was dead and gone.
B7
(A7)
F#7
(E7)
I was think-in' a - bout you, ba - by,
E7/G#
(D7/F#)
B
(A)
B7/A
(A7/G)
E/G#
(D/F#)
Em/G
(Dm/F)
B/F#
(A/E)
F#7
(E7)
why you hear me weep and moan.
2. I got dead
Verse
B7
(A7)
B°7
(A°7)
shrimps here.
Some-one is fish-in' in my pond.

B7
(A7)
B°7
(A°7)
B7
(A7)
E7/G#
(D7/F#)
I got dead shrimps he' - ooh.
Some - one fish-in' in my pond.
B7
(A7)
B°7
(A°7)
B7
(A7)
I've served
F#7
(E7)
E7/G#
(D7/F#)
B
(A)
B7/A
(A7/G)
E/G#
(D/F#)
Em/G
(Dm/F)
my best bait ba - by, and I can't do that no harm.
Verse
B/F#
(A/E)
F#7
(E7)
B7
(A7)
B°7
(A°7)
3. K, ev-'ry-thing I do, babe, you got your mouth stuck out.

B7 (A7)
B°7 (A°7)
B7 (A7)
B°7 (A°7)
B7 (A7)
Hole where I used to fish, you got me post - ed out. Ev - 'ry - thing
E7/G♯ (D7/F♯)
B7 (A7)
B°7 (A°7)
I do, you got your mouth stuck out.
B7 (A7)
F♯7 (E7)
E7/G♯ (D7/F♯)
At the hole where I used to fish, ba - by, you've got me post - ed out.
B (A)
B7/A (A7/G)
E/G♯ (D/F♯)
Em/G (Dm/F)
B/F♯ (A/E)
F♯7 (E7)
Verse
B7 (A7)
4. I got dead shrimps here 'n'

B°7
(A°7)
B7
(A7)
B°7
(A°7)
B7
(A7)
some-one fish-in' in my pond.
I got
E7/G♯
(D7/F♯)
B7
(A7)
B°7
(A°7)
dead shrimps here,
some-one fish-in' in my pond.
B7
(A7)
F♯7
(E7)
E7/G♯
(D7/F♯)
Catch-in' my gog-gle-eye perch-es,
and they bar-be-cu-in' the bone.
B/F♯
(A/E)
B7/A
(A7/G)
E/G♯
(D/F♯)
Em/G
(Dm/F)
B/F♯
(A/E)
F♯7
(E7)
Verse
B7
(A7)
5. Now you take my shrimp, ba-by. You

B°7
(A°7)
B7
(A7)
know you turned me down.
I could-n't do noth-in' un-til I got my-
-self un-wound.
You tak-en my shrimp,
ohh,
know you turned me down.
E7/G#
(D7/F#)
Babe, I could-n't do noth-in'
F#7
(E7)
un-til I got my-self un-wound.
B
(A)
B7/A
(A7/G)
E/G# Em/G
(D/F#)(Dm/F)

# Cross Road Blues (Crossroads)

SA 2629 - 2

Words and Music by Robert Johnson

* Tunings were determined using the original 78s. To play along with the *Robert Johnson - The Complete Recordings* CD set, Capo III.

E7
(D7)
I went to the cross - road,
w/o slide
1/4
B
(A)
fell down on my knees.
w/ slide
w/o slide
F#7
(E7)
Asked the Lord a - bove, "Have mer - cy.
B
(A)
B7
(A7)
Save poor Bob, if you please."
1/2

Verse
B
(A)
B
(A)
2. Mmm, stand-in' at the cross - road,
w/ slide
w/o slide
I tried to flag a ride.
w/ slide
w/o slide
B7
(A7)
Stand-in' at the cross -
1/2
E7
(D7)
- road,
I tried to flag a ride.
1/4
1/4
1/4

B
(A)
B7
(A7)
w/ slide
1/2
F#7
(E7)
Did - n't no - bod - y seem to know me. Ev - 'ry -
w/ slide
B7
(A7)
bod - y pass me by.
w/o slide
1/4
1/4
B
(A)
Verse
B
(A)
3. Mmm, the sun go - in' down, boy.
w/ slide

Dark _ gon' _ catch me here.
w/o slide
w/ slide
E7
(D7)
Ooo _ eee,
w/o slide
1/4
B7
(A7)
boy, dark gon' catch me here.
1/4
1/4
w/ slide
I have - n't
w/o slide
1/2

F#7#9
(E7#9)
got no lov - in' sweet wom - an that
B7
(A7)
love and feel my care.
w/ slide
w/o slide
B
(A)
4. You can
Verse
B
(A)
run, you can run.
Tell my friend - boy Wil - lie Brown.
w/ slide
w/o slide
B7
(A7)
You can

E7
(D7)
run,
tell my friend - boy Wil - lie Brown.
B
(A)
Lord, that I'm
w/ slide
w/o slide
F#7#9
(E7#9)
B7
(A7)
stand - in' at the cross - road, babe,
I be - -lieve I'm sink - in' down.
w/ slide
w/o slide
B
(A)
w/ slide

# Walkin' Blues

SA 2630 - 1

Words and Music by Robert Johnson

* Tunings were determined using the original 78s. To play along with the *Robert Johnson - The Complete Recordings* CD set, Capo III.

B
(A)
feel-in' 'round oh, for my shoes. _ But you _ know _
w/o slide
w/ slide
w/o slide
w/ slide
* w/o slide
w/ slide
* downstemmed note only
E7
(D7)
F#7
(E7)
E7
(D7)
'bout 'at I got these old walk - in' blues.
w/o slide
w/ slide
B
(A)
Verse
B
(A)
2. Lord, I feel like blow - in' my
* w/o slide
w/ slide
w/o slide
w/ slide
* downstemmed note only
woh-old lone - some ho'n. _ Got up this morn-in', my lit - tle Ber -

E7
(D7)
- nice was gone. Lord, I feel like blow-ooon' my lone-some ho'n.
w/o slide
B
(A)
E7
(D7)
Well, I got up this morn - in'
w/ slide
w/o slide
w/ slide
F#7
(E7)
E7
(D7)
B
(A)
woh - all I had was gone.
3. Well,-ah,
w/o slide
w/ slide
w/o slide
w/ slide
Verse
B
(A)
leave this morn' if I have to woh, ride the blind, ah. I've feel mis - treat - ed and I

E7
(D7)
don't mind dy'n'. Leav-in' this morn', ah, I have to ride a blind.
w/o slide
w/ slide
B
(A)
F#7
(E7)
Babe, I been mis-treat-ed, ba-
w/o slide
w/ slide
w/o slide
E7
(D7)
B
(A)
- by and I don't mind dy-in'.
4. Well,
1/4
w/ slide
w/o slide
w/ slide
Verse
B
(A)
some peo-ple tell me that the wor-ried blues ain't bad.

E7
(D7)
Worst old feel-in' I most ev - er had. Some peo - ple tell me that these
w/o slide
* Snap str. against fingerboard.
B
(A)
old wor-ried old blues ain't bad. It's the
w/ slide
w/o slide
w/ slide
w/o slide
w/ slide
F#7
(E7)
E7
(D7)
B
(A)
worst old feel - in' I most ev - er had.
w/o slide
w/ slide
Verse
B
(A)
5. She got a El - gin move-ment from her head down

to her toes.
Break in on a dol - lar most an - y -
E7
(D7)
where she goes.
Ooo,
to her head down to her toes.
* w/o slide
w/o slide
* downstemmed note only
B
(A)
F#7
(E7)
Spoken: Oh, honey.
Lord, she break in on a dol - lar most
w/ slide
w/o slide
w/ slide
w/o slide
E7
(D7)
B
(A)
an - y - where she goes.
w/ slide

# Last Fair Deal Gone Down

SA 2631 - 1

Words and Music by Robert Johnson

* Tunings were determined using the original 78s. To play along with the *Robert Johnson - The Complete Recordings* CD set, Capo I.

Editor's Note: In the re-tuning process, Robert's guitar progressively became sharper in pitch with each of the previous three songs until he became 1/4 step sharp.

down, good Lord, on that Gulf - port Is - land Road.
w/o slide
w/ slide
w/o slide
A7/G D/F# Dm/F A/E A
Verse
A
2. Eh, I - da Belle, don't cry this
w/ slide
time. I - da Belle, don't cry this time. If you
w/o slide
w/ slide
cry a - bout a nick - el, you'll die 'bout a dime. She would-n't

A7/G D/F♯ Dm/F A/E A
Verse
A
cry, but the mon - ey won't mind.
3. I like y' way you
w/o slide
w/ slide
w/o slide
w/ slide
w/o slide
w/ slide
do. I love the way you do. I
love the way you do, good Lord, on this
w/o slide
A7/G Dm/F A
Gulf - port Is - land Road.
4. My
w/ slide
w/o slide

Verse

A
cap - tain's so mean on me. My
w/ slide
w/o slide
w/ slide
cap - tain's so mean on me. My
w/o slide
w/ slide
cap - tain's so mean on m' mmm, good Lord, on this
w/o slide
A7/G D/F# A/E A
Gulf - port Is - land Road. 5. They
w/ slide
w/o slide

Verse
A7
count, they pick and sing.
Count, they pick and
sing.
Let's count and pick and
sing, good Lord, on that
w/ slide
A7/G
D/F#
A/E
Gulf - port Is - land Road.
6. Ah, this
w/o slide
Verse
A
last fair deal go - in' down.
It's the last fair deal go - in' down.
w/ slide
w/o slide
w/ slide

This' the last fair deal go - in' down, good Lord, on this
w/o slide
A7/G D/F♯ Dm/F A/E
Verse
A
Gulf - port Is - land Road.
7. I'm work - in' my way back home.
w/ slide
w/o slide
w/ slide
I'm work - in' my way back home.
I'm
w/o slide
w/ slide
work - in' my way back home, good Lord, on this Gulf - port Is - land Road.

Verse
A7/G D/F# A
A
8. And that thing don't keep a-ring - in' so soon.
w/o slide
w/ slide
Harm.
w/o slide
That thing don't keep a-ring - in' so soon.
Harm.
w/ slide
And that thing don't keep a-ring - in' so soon, good Lord, on that
Harm.
w/o slide
w/ slide
w/o slide
A7/G D/F# Dm/F A/E
Gulfed and Port Is - land Road.
w/ slide
w/o slide
w/ slide

# Preachin' Blues (Up Jumped the Devil)

SA 2632 - 1

Words and Music by Robert Johnson

* Tunings were determined using the original 78s. To play along with the *Robert Johnson - The Complete Recordings* CD set, Capo I.
Editor's Note: Just like the previous song, "Last Fair Deal Gone Down," Robert's guitar was 1/4 step sharp for this recording.

I's up this morn', ah,
w/o slide
w/ slide
w/o slide
blues walk-in' like a man.
w/ slide
Wor-ried blues, give me your right hand.
w/o slide
w/ slide
2. And the

Verse
E7
blues fell, ma-ma's child,
tore all up-side down.
w/o slide
w/ slide
w/o slide
w/ slide
w/o slide w/ slide
Blues
fell, ma-ma's child,
and it tore me all up-side down.
w/o slide
w/ slide
Tra-vel on, poor Bob,
w/o slide
w/ slide

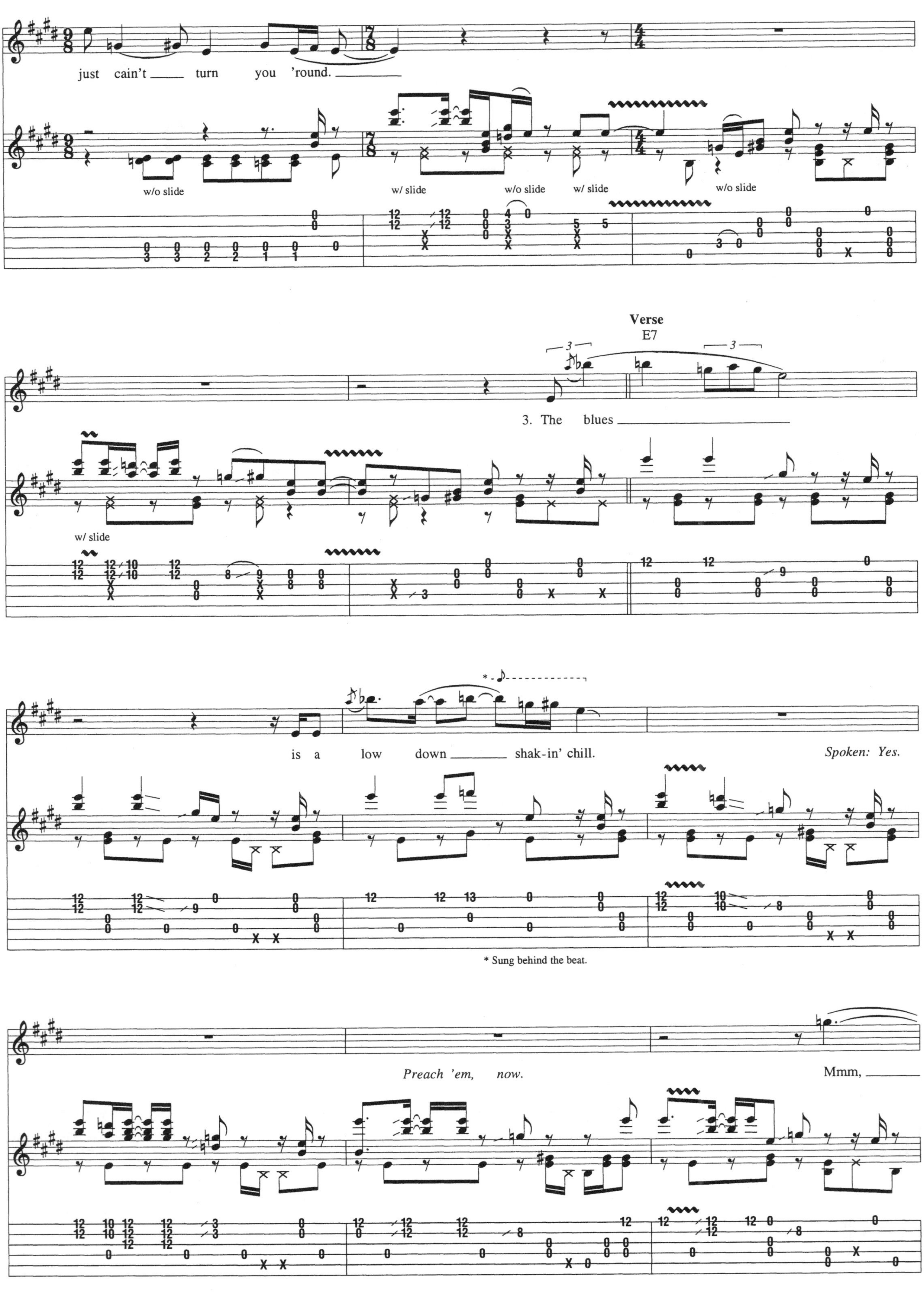

just cain't turn you 'round.

w/o slide w/ slide w/o slide w/ slide w/o slide

**Verse**

E7

3. The blues

w/ slide

* Sung behind the beat.

is a low - down shak-in' chill.
w/o slide
w/ slide
1/4
You ain't nev-er had 'em, I
hope you nev - er will.
4. Well, the blues

Verse
E7
is a ach - in' old heart di - sease.
w/o slide
w/ slide
w/o slide
w/ slide
Spoken: Do it, now.
w/o slide
You gon-na do it? Tell me all a-
w/ slide
w/o slide
w/ slide
w/o slide
w/ slide
w/o slide
bout it. Let the blues is a
w/ slide

low - down, ach - in' heart _ di- sease.
w/o slide
Like con - sump - tion, kil-ling me ___ by de - grees.
w/ slide
w/o slide
5. I can
w/ slide
Verse
E7
stud-y rain, ___ oh, oh, __ drive, oh, __

— oh, drive — my blues.
I been studyin' the rain and I 'on'
w/o slide
w/ slide
w/o slide
drive — my blues a - way. –
w/ slide
Go-in' to the 'stil - 'ry, stay out there all day. —
w/o slide
w/ slide
w/o slide
w/ slide

# If I Had Possession over Judgment Day

SA 2633 - 1

Words and Music by Robert Johnson

* Tunings were determined using the original 78s. To play along with the *Robert Johnson - The Complete Recordings* CD set, Capo I.
Editor's Note: Just like the previous song, "Preaching Blues," Robert's guitar was 1/4 step sharp for this recording.

D
pos - ses - sion
o - ver judg - ment day,
A
Lord, the
w/o slide
w/ slide
w/o slide
E
D
lit - tle wom - an I'm lov - in' would - n't
have no right to pray.
w/ slide
* Sung behind the beat.
A
w/o slide
w/ slide
w/o slide
w/ slide

Verse
A
2. And I went to the moun - tain, look-in' far as my eyes could see.
w/o slide
w/ slide
And I went to the moun - tain, look-in' far as my eye would see.
Some oth - er man

E
D
got my wom-an and the' - a, lone - some blues got me.

A
w/o slide
w/ slide

**Verse**

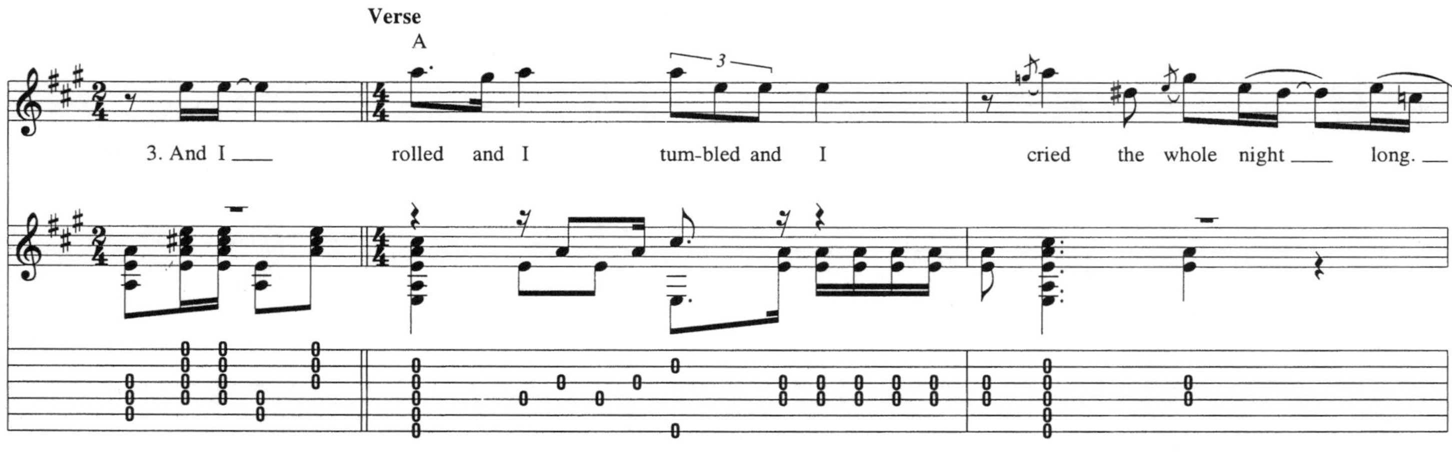
A
3. And I rolled and I tum-bled and I cried the whole night long.

w/o slide
w/ slide

D
And I rolled and I tum - bled and I cried the whole night long.
A
Boy, I woke up
E
this morn - in', my bis - cuit rol - ler gone.
A
w/ slide
w/o slide

Verse
A
4. Had to fold my arms and I slow-ly walked a - way.
w/ slide
Spoken: I didn't like the way she done.
w/o slide
w/ slide
w/o slide
w/ slide
Had to fold my arms and I
slow - ly walked a - way.
w/o slide
w/ slide

D
E
D
I said in my mind, "Yo' trou-ble gon' come some - day."
A
w/o slide
w/ slide
Verse
A
Now run here, ba - by, set down on my knee.
w/o slide
w/ slide
w/o slide
w/ slide
Now,

run here, ba - by, set down on my, on my
8va
steady gliss.
*
** Position slide where imaginary fret would be.
knee.
loco
w/o slide
E
D
I wan-na tell you all a - bout the way they treat - ed me.
w/ slide
A
A7/G D/F# Dm/F A/E A
w/o slide
w/ slide
w/o slide
w/ slide

# Stones in My Passway

DAL 377 - 2

Words and Music by Robert Johnson

Open A Tuning:
①=E ④=E
②=C♯ ⑤=A
③=A ⑥=E

Intro

Moderately ♩ = 92

*A7

1. I got

*mf*
w/ slide
w/ fingers

w/o slide

*Chord symbols reflect implied tonality.

A7
E7#9
D7
I have pains in my heart. _ They have _
w/ slide
A7
___ tak-en my ap - pe-tite. _
2. I have a
w/o slide
Verse
A7
bird ___ to whis - tle ___ and I _ have a bird to sing. ______
D7
Have a bird to whis - tle ___ and I have a bird to sing. ______
1/4

A7
E7#9
D7
I got a wom-an that I'm lov-in', boy,
w/ slide
but she don't mean a thing.
3. My en-e-mies
w/o slide
Verse
have be-trayed me,
have o-ver-tak-en poor Bob at last.
My en-e-mies have be-trayed me,

A7
have o-ver-tak-en poor Bob at last.
An' 'ere's
1/4
1/4

E7#9
D7
A7
one thing cer-tain-ly, they have stones all in my pass.
w/ slide
w/o slide
1/4

Bridge
A7
Now you try-in' to take my life and all my lov-in', too.

You laid a pass-way for me. Now what are you try - ing to do? I'm cry - in' please,

*Tap finger on guitar body.

D7
I got three legs to truck home.
1/4
1/4

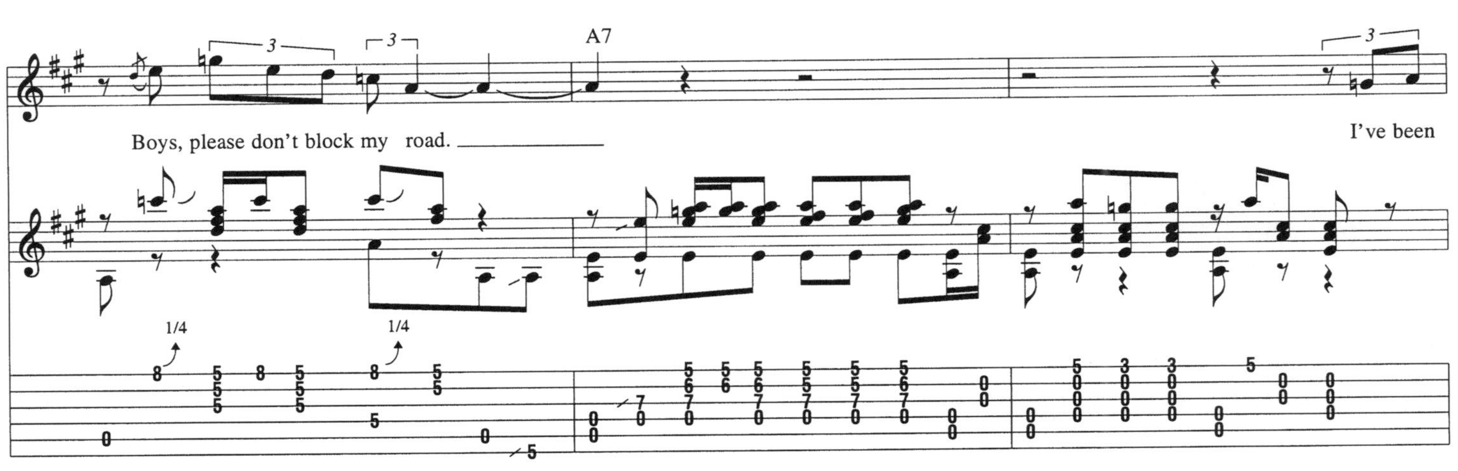
A7
Boys, please don't block my road.
I've been
1/4
1/4

E7#9
D7
feel-in' a-shamed 'bout my rid - er.
Babe, I'm booked and I got to go.
w/ slide
w/o slide

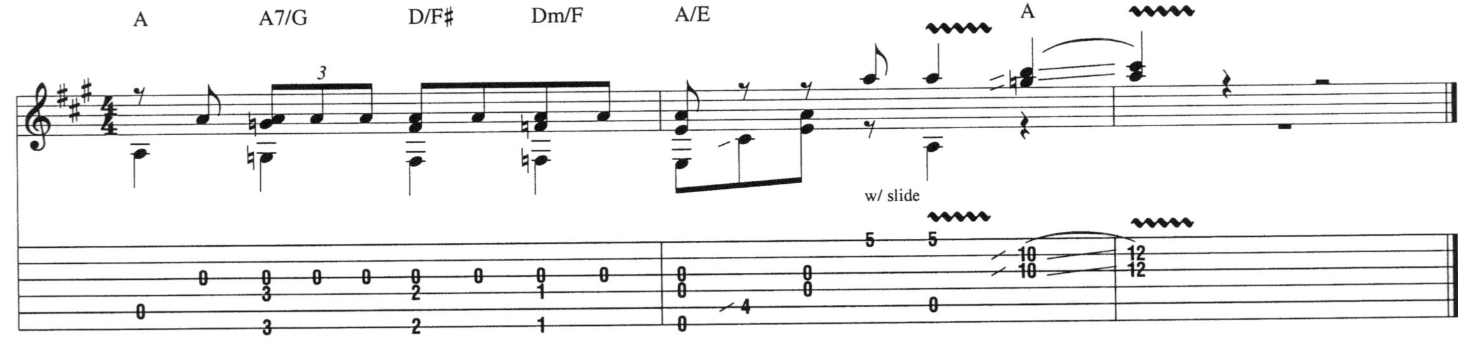
A
A7/G
D/F#
Dm/F
A/E
A
w/ slide

# I'm a Steady Rollin' Man (Steady Rollin' Man)

DAL 378 - 1

Words and Music by Robert Johnson

E7
D7
have-n't got no sweet wom-an, hmm, mmm, boys, to be roll-in' this-a way.
* downstem double stop played with 3rd finger of left hand
A7
Verse
A7
2. I'm the man that rolls
1/4
when ic - i-cles is hang-in' on the tree.
I'm the man
1/4
D7
A7
that roll
when ic - i-cles is hang-in' on the tree.
1/4

E7
And now you hear me howl - in', ba - by, hmm,
D7
A7
down on my bend-ed knee.
3. I'm a hard
Verse
A7
work-in' man,
have been for man-y years, I know.
D7
I'm a hard work-in' man,
have been for man-y long years, I know.
1/4

A7
E7
And some cream puff's us - in' my mon-ey, ooh, well babe,
D7
A7
but that-'ll nev-er be no more.
4. You can't give
Verse
A7
your sweet wom - an ev - 'ry - thing she wants in one time.
D7
Ooh, hoo, ooo, you can't give your sweet wom-an

A7
ev-'ry-thing she wants in one time.
Well boys,
E7
D7
she get ramb-lin' in her brain, hmm, some mon-key man on her mind.
A7
5. I'm a stead-
Verse
A7
y roll-in' man; I roll both night and day.

D7
I'm a steady-y roll-in' man,
A7
and I roll both night and day.
Well, I
E7
don't have no sweet wom - an,
hmm,
boys,
D7
to be roll - in' this - a way.
A7
E7
A
A7/G
D/F# Dm/F
E7
A
1/4
* discontinue P M

# From Four Until Late

DAL 379 - 1

Words and Music by Robert Johnson

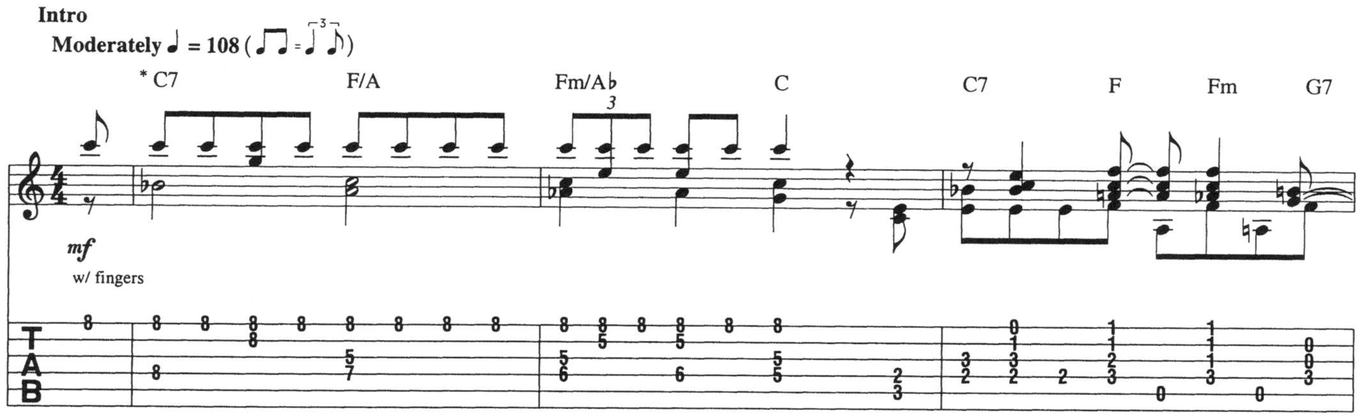


* Chord symbols reflect implied tonality.

** Fret 5th & 6th strings with 3rd finger of left hand.

*** downstem notes only

Fm7
C
A7/E
in' my hands and cry - in'.
I be - lieve
D7/F♯
G7
C
C7
F
Fm7
to my soul that your dad - dy's Gulf - port bound.
Verse
G
C
F
2. From Mem - phis to Nor - folk is a thir - ty - six hours' ride.
C
C7
F
From Mem - phis to Nor - folk is a thir -

Fm7
C
A7
ty - six hours' ride.
A man is
D7/F#
G7
C
C7
F
Fm7
like a pris-on-er and he's nev - er sat - is - fied.
Verse
C/E
G7
C
F
3. A wom-an is like a dres-ser, some man al-ways ramb-lin' th'ough its drawers.
C
C7
F
A wom-an is like a dres-ser, some man's

Fm7
C
always rambling' th'ough its drawers.
A7
D7/F#
G7
It cause so many men wear an apron overhall.
C
C7
F
Fm7
C
G7
Verse
C
4. From four until late, she get with a
* Played and sung slightly ahead of the beat.
F
C
C7
no-good bunch and clown.
From four

F
Fm7
until late, she get with a no-good bunch and clown.
C
A7
D7/F#
Now she won't do nothin' but tear a good
G
C7
F
Fm7
C/E
G7
man' rep-u-ta-tion down.
5. When I leave
Verse
C
F
this town, I'm 'on' bid you fare... fare-well.

C
C7
F7
And when I leave this town, I'm gon' bid
you fare... fare - well.
C
A7
And when I re -
D7/F#
G
C7
F
Fm7
turn a - gain, you'll have a great long stor - y to tell.
G7
C
C7/B♭
F/A
Fm/A♭
C
C7

# Hell Hound on My Trail

Open Em Tuning:
① = E ④ = E
② = B ⑤ = B
③ = G ⑥ = E

DAL 394 - 2
Words and Music by Robert Johnson

Intro
Moderately ♩ = 88

*E7 E°7 Am E E7/D A/C♯ Am/C

mf
w/ fingers

*Chord symbols reflect implied tonality.

E7

Verse
E B7

1. I got to keep mov - in', I've got to keep mov - in',

E E7 A/C♯ Am/C E7

blues fall - in' down like hail. Blues fall - in' down like hail.

Mmm, blues fall - in' down like hail.

Editor's Note: The pickup note, along with beat two of the fourth measure are on the original 78, but were somehow lost when the *Robert Johnson - The Complete Recordings,* CD set was produced.

E7 A/C# Am/C E E7 A/C# E7
Blues fall-in' down like hail. And the day,
B7
it keeps on wor-'y'n' me. It's a hell hound on my trail,
E E7/D A/C# Am/C E E7/D A/C# Am/C
hell hound on my trail. Hell hound on my trail,
E7
Verse
E
2. If to-day was Christ-mas Eve, if to-day

B7
was Christ-mas Eve,
and to-mor-row was Christ-mas Day.
E
E7/D
A/C#
E7
If to-day was Christ-mas Eve,
and to-mor-row was Christ-mas Day.
A/C#
Am/C
Spoken: Aow, wouldn't we have a time, baby?
E7
B7
All I would need, my lit-tle sweet rid-er just

E7/D
A/C#
Am/C
E
to pass the time a-way.
Huh huh,
to pass the time a-way.
E/B
E7
Verse
3. You sprin-kl-ed hot foot pow-der, mmm,
a-round my door,
all a-round my door.
You sprin-kl-ed hot foot pow-der
all a-round your dad-y's door.
1/4

E7/D A/C♯ Am/C E/B E7
Hmm, hmm, hmm.
It keep me with a
B7
ram-blin' mind, rid - er,
ev-'ry old place I go,
E E7/D A/C♯ Am/C
ev-'ry old place I go.
E E7 A/C♯ Am/C E7
Verse
E
4. I can tell the wind is ris - in'
the leaves tremb-lin' on the tree,
E7/D A/C♯ Am/C
tremb-lin' on the tree.

E/B
E7
I can tell the wind is ris - in',
leaves tremb-lin' on the tree.
E7/D
A/C#
Am/C
E/B
E
E7
Hmm, hmm, hmm.
B7
All I need's my lit - tle sweet wom - an and to keep my com - pan - y.
E
E7/D
A/C#
Am/C
E
E7/D
A/C#
Am/C
E7
Hey, my com-pan-y.

# Little Queen of Spades

DAL 395 - 1

Words and Music by Robert Johnson

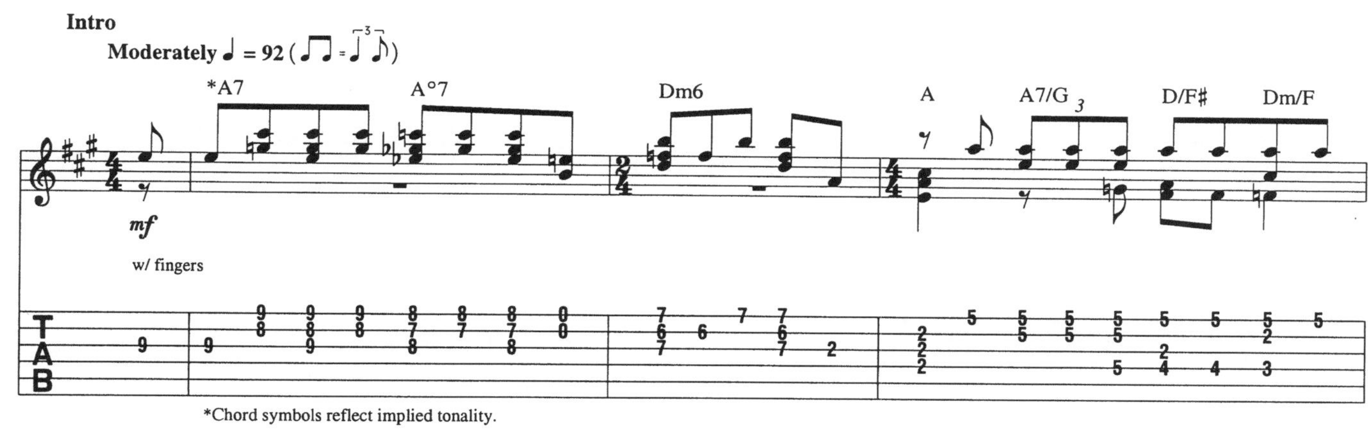


*Chord symbols reflect implied tonality.

**downstem notes only, except during the turnarounds

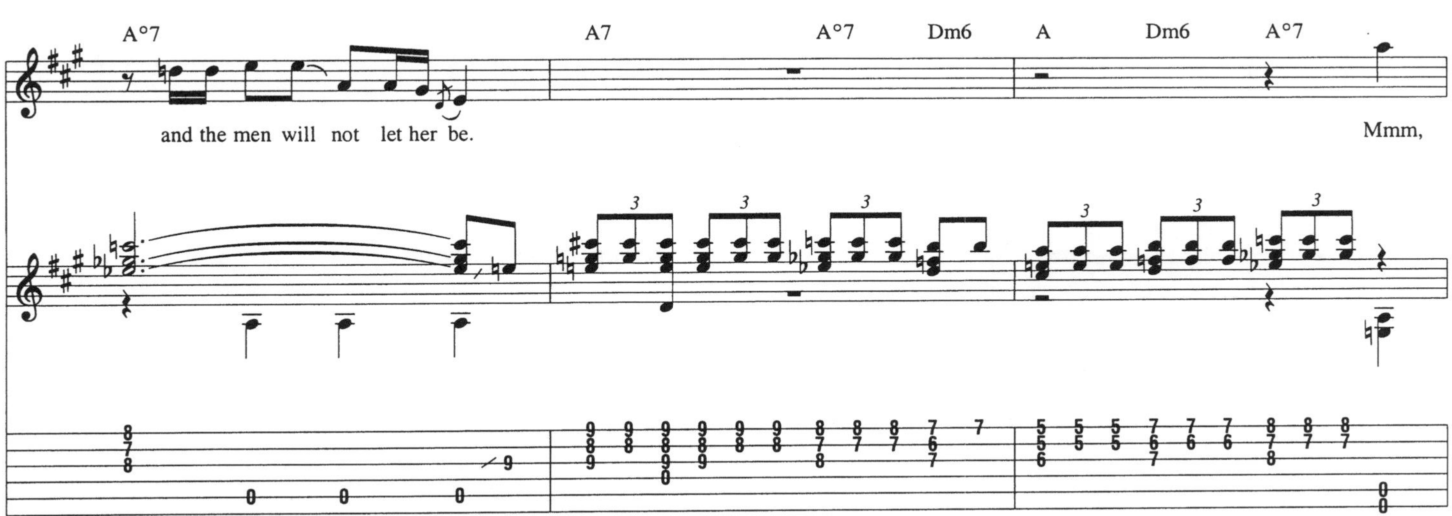


* Tunings were determined using the original 78s. To play along with the *Robert Johnson - The Complete Recordings* CD set, tune 1/4 step sharp.

D7/F♯
mmm, she is the lit - tle queen of spades
and the men will not let her be.
A7
E7
Ev-'ry - time she makes a spread, hoo, fair brown
D7/F♯
A
A7/G
D/F♯
Dm/F
A/E
E7
cold chill just runs all o - ver me.
Verse
A7
A°7
2. I'm gon' get me a gamb-lin' wom - an,
if the last thing that I do.

A7 A°7 Dm6 A Dm6 A°7 A7 D7/F#
Eee, hee, _ gon' get me a gamb-lin' wom-an ___
if it's the last thing that I do. ___
A7 A°7 A7
Well, a
E7 D7/F#
man don't need a wom-an, ___ hoo, fair brown, _ that he got to give all ___ his ___ mon-ey to. ___
A A7/G D/F# Dm/F A/E E7
Verse
A7
3. Ev-'ry - bod-y say she got a mo - jo,

A°7
A7
A°7
Dm6
A°7
Dm6
A°7
now she's been us-in' that stuff.
Mmm, mmm,
D7/F#
'vry-bod-y says she got a mo-jo
'cause she been us-in' that stuff.
A7
A°7
A7
But she got a way trim-min' down,
hoo, fair
E7
D7/F#
brown, and I mean it's most too tough.
A
A7/G
D/F#
Dm/F
A/E
E7
4. Now, lit-tle

Verse
A7
A°7
Dm6
girl, since I'm am the King, ba-by, and you is a queen.
A
Dm6
D7/F#
Ooo, hoo, eee, since I am the King, ba-by, and you is a queen.
E7
Le's us put our heads to-geth-er, hoo,
A7/G
D/F# Dm/F
fair brown, then we can make our mon-ey green.

# Malted Milk

DAL 396 - 1

Words and Music by Robert Johnson

* Drop D Tuning:
① = E ④ = D
② = B ⑤ = A
③ = G ⑥ = D

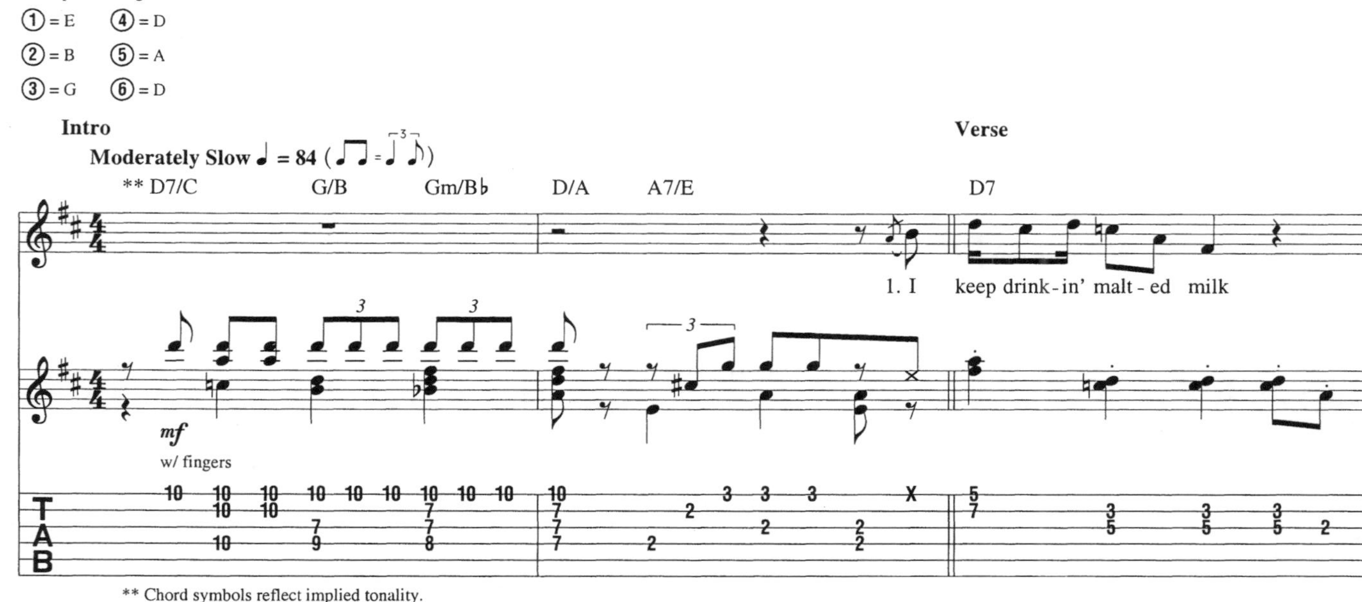


** Chord symbols reflect implied tonality.

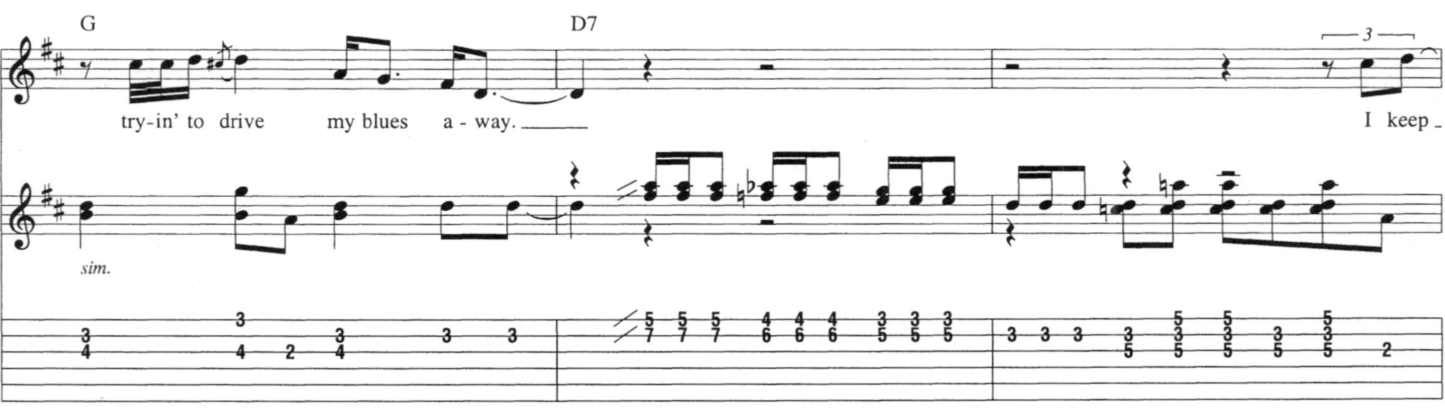

* Tunings were determined using the original 78s. To play along with the *Robert Johnson - The Complete Recordings* CD set, Capo I.

D7
Ba - by, you just as
1/2
A7
wel - come to my lov - in'
as the
G
flow - ers is in May.
D
C°7
B°7
A7
Verse
D7
2. Malt - ed milk, malt - ed milk
G
keep rush - in' to my head.
D7
Malt -
sim.

G
D7
ed milk, malt - ed milk
keep rush - in' to my head.
A7
And I have a fun-ny, fun-ny feel - in' and I'm
G
D B7 B♭7 A7
talk - in' all out my head.
Ba - by, fix
Verse
D7 G D7
me one more drink and hug your dad - dy one more time.
sim.

G
Ba-by, fix me one more drink and hug your dad-dy one more time.
D7
D
Keep on stir-rin'
A7
G
in my malt - ed milk, ma - ma, un - til I change my mind.
D
B7
B♭7
A7
Verse
D7
4. My door - knob keeps on turn-in'; it

G
D
D7
must be spook's a - round _ my bed. ______
My
G
D
door-knob keeps on turn - in'; _____
must be spooks a-round my bed. ___
A7
I have a warm, ____ old __ feel-in' and the hair __
G7
D7
rit.
D
___ ris - in' on my head. ___
rit.

# Drunken Hearted Man

DAL 397 - 1

Words and Music by Robert Johnson

* Tunings were determined using the original 78s. To play along with the *Robert Johnson - The Complete Recordings* CD set, Capo I.
Editor's Note: Robert's guitar was 1/4 step sharp for this recording.

D
And if I could change
A
G
D/A
B7/F♯
B♭7/F
my way of liv-in', it t'would mean so much to me.
P.M.
A7/E
Verse
D7
G
2. I been dogged and I been driv-en eve' since I left my moth-er's home.
D
Gm
D
D7
G
I been dogged and I been driv-en eve'

D
since I left my moth-er's home.
And I can't see the
* Sung behind the beat.
A7
G
rea - son why that I can't leave these no good wom-ens a - lone.
P.M.
D/A B7/F# Bb7/F A7/E
Verse
D7
3. My fath - er died and left me. My poor
G
D
moth - er done the best that she could.

* Played as even eighth notes

D
D7
G
Spoken: Oh, play 'em, now.
I'm a drunk - en heart - ed man
P.M.
D
and sin was the cause of it all.
And the day that you
P.M.
A7
G
get weak for no - good wom - en, that's the day that you're bound to fall.
A°
G♯°
A7
D
G/B
Gm/B♭
A7
D7
P.M.
1/4
1/4

# Me and the Devil Blues

DAL 398 - 1

Words and Music by Robert Johnson

Tunings were determined using the original 78s. To play along with the *Robert Johnson - The Complete Recordings* CD set, Capo I.
Editor's Note: Just like the previous song, "Drunken Hearted Man," Robert's guitar was 1/4 step sharp for this recording.

A7
A°7 A7
when you knocked up - on my door,
and I
E7
D7/F#
A
A7/G
D/F#
Dm/F
said, "Hel-lo, Sa - tan.
I be-lieve it's time to go."
Verse
A/E
E7
A7
A°7
A7
A°7
2. Me and the Dev - il
was walk-in' side by side.
Harm.
Harm.
* Fretted with last 3 fingers.
A7
A°7
A7
A°7
A7
D7
Me and the Dev - il, ooh,

A7
A°7
A7
was walk-in' side by side.
And I'm go - in'
1/4 1/4 1/4
E7
D7/F#
A A7/G D/F# Dm/F
to beat my wom-an
un-til I get sat - is - fied.
Verse
A/E E7
A7
A°7
A7
A°7
3. She say, "You don't see why
that you will dog me 'round."
A7
A°7
A7
A°7
A7
Spoken: Now babe, you know you ain't doin' me right, don' cha?
She say, "You

D7/F#
don't see why, ooh,
that you will dog me 'round."
A7
A°7
A7
It must-a be that old e-vil spir-it
E7
D7/F#
so deep down in the ground.
A
A7/G
D/F#
Dm/F
A/E
E7
Verse
4. You may bur-y my bod-y
Harm.
A7
A°7
down by the high-way side.
*Spoken: Baby, I don't care where you bury my body when I'm dead and gone.*

A7
A°7
A7
D7/F♯
You may bur - y my bod - y, ooh,
A7
A°7
A7
down by the high - way side
so my old e - vil
E7
D7/F♯
spir - it
can catch a Grey - hound bus and ride.
A
A7/G
D/F♯
Dm/F
E7
A

# Stop Breakin' Down Blues

DAL 399 - 1

Words and Music by Robert Johnson

* Open A Tuning:

① = E ④ = E

② = C# ⑤ = A

③ = A ⑥ = E

* Tunings were determined using the original 78s. To play along with the *Robert Johnson - The Complete Recordings* CD set, Capo I.
Editor's Note: Just like the previous song, "Me & The Devil Blues," Robert's guitar was 1/4 step sharp for this recording.

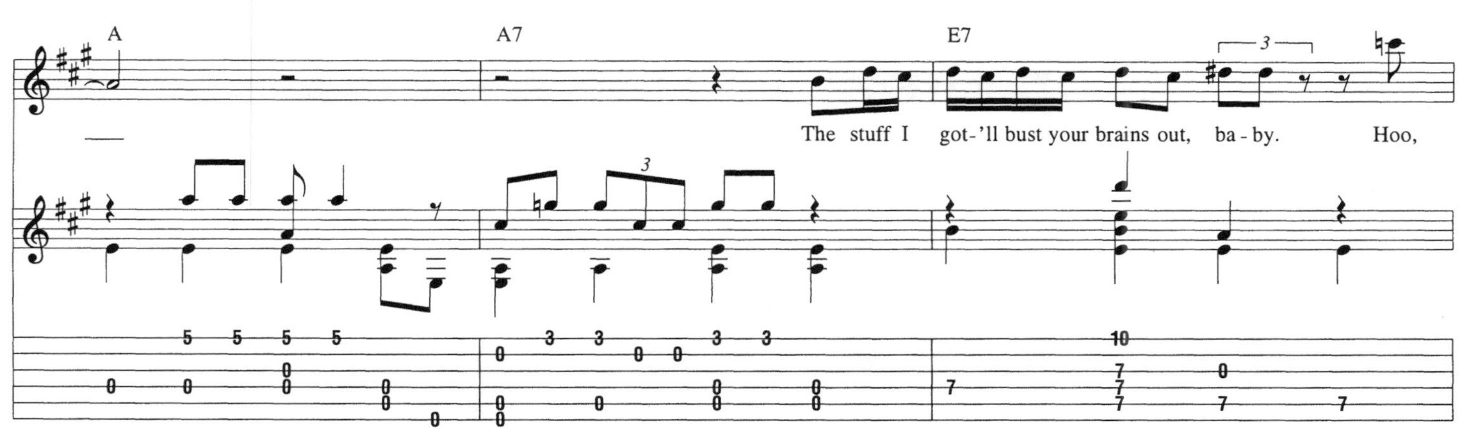
A
A7
E7
The stuff I got-'ll bust your brains out, ba-by. Hoo,

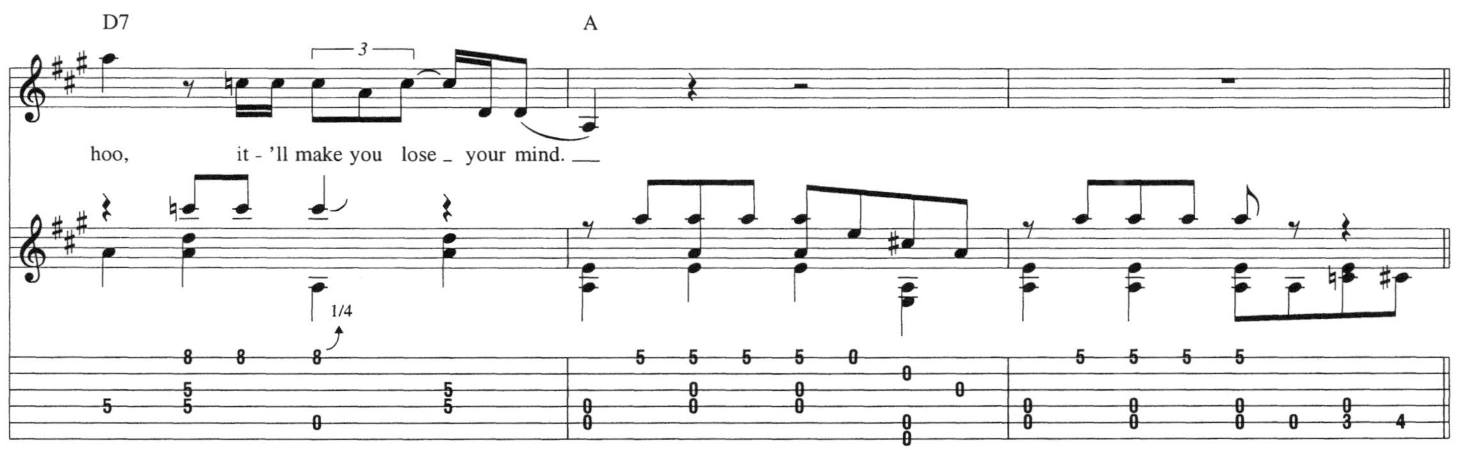
D7
A
hoo, it-'ll make you lose your mind.
1/4

**Verse**

A
2. I can't walk the streets, now, con... con-sol-ate my mind.

Some no good wom-an, she starts break-in' down. Stop break-in'

D7
A
down.
Please, stop break - in' down.
1/4
1/4
A7
E7
The stuff I got, it gon' bust your brains out. Hoo,
1/4
D7
A
hoo, it - 'll make you lose your mind.
1/4
1/2
Verse
A
3. Now, you Sat - ur - day night wom - ens,

you love to ape and clown.
You won't do noth - in' but tear a good man
rep - u - ta - tion down.
Stop break - in' down.
D7
Please, stop break - in' down.
A
A7
The stuff
E7
I got - 'll bust your brains out, ba - by.
D7
Hoo, hoo, it - 'll make you lose your mind.

A
A7
A
Verse
A
4. Now, I give my ba - by, now, the
nine - ty - nine de - gree.
She jumped up and throwed a pis - tol
down on me. Stop break - in' down.
D7
1/4

A
A7
Please, stop break - in' down.
Stuff I
E7
D7
got - 'll bust your brains out, ba - by.
Hoo, hoo, it - 'll make you lose your mind.
A
Verse
A
5. I can't start walk - in'
A7
A
down the streets.
But some pret - ty ma - ma don't start break -

A7
D7
in' down with me.
Stop break - in' down.
1/4
A
A7
Yes, stop break - in' down.
The stuff I
1/4
1/4
E7
D7
got - 'll bust your brains out, ba - by.
Hoo, hoo, it - 'll make you lose your mind.
1/4
1/4
A/E
A7/G
D/F#
Dm/F
A/E
A
w/ slide
* discontinue P.M.

# Traveling Riverside Blues

DAL 400 - 1
Words and Music by Robert Johnson

* Tunings were determined using the original 78s. To play along with the *Robert Johnson - The Complete Recordings* CD set, Capo I.
Editor's Note: In the re-tuning process, Robert's guitar progressively became sharper with each of the previous three songs until he became nearly 1/2 step sharp.

A
want you have your fun,
w/o slide
w/ slide
w/o slide
w/ slide
w/o slide
w/ slide
w/o slide
E
D
E
come on back to Friar's Point, ma - ma, bar - rel-house all night long.
w/ slide
A
2. I got wom-ens
w/o slide
w/ slide
w/o slide
w/ slide
w/o slide
w/ slide
Verse
A
in Vicks-burg, clean on in - to Ten - nes - see,
w/o slide
w/ slide
w/o slide

I got wom-ens in Vicks-burg,
w/ slide
w/o slide
clear on in - to Ten - nes - see,
but my Friar's Point rid - er, now, she hops all o - ver me.
D
E
A
3. I ain't gon - na

Verse
A
state no col - or, but her front teeth is crowned with gold.
w/ slide
I ain't gon-na
w/o slide
w/ slide
w/o slide
B7
A7
state no col - or, but her front teeth crowned with gold.
A
She got a lien

D
E
A
on my bod-y, now and a mort - gage on my soul.
w/ slide
w/o slide
w/ slide
w/o slide
* Sung behind the beat.
Verse
A
4. Now, I'm go - in' to Rose - dale,
take my rid - er by my side.
Lord, I'm go - in' to Rose - dale an' take my rid - er by my side.

Ah, we gon'
w/ o slide
w/ slide
w/ o slide
D
E
bar - rel - house all night long, 'cause it's on the riv - er - side.
w/ slide
A
5. Now, you may squeeze
w/o slide
w/ slide
w/o slide
w/ slide
w/o slide
w/ slide
Verse
A
my lem-on 'til the juice runs down my leg.
w/o slide
w/ slide
w/o slide

You may squeeze my lem - on 'til the
w/ slide
w/o slide
w/ slide
w/o slide
w/ slide
juice runs down my leg.
w/o slide
w/ slide
w/o slide
w/ slide
w/o slide
w/ slide
w/o slide
D
E
Babe, I'm go - in' back to Friars Point if I be rock - in' to my head.
w/ slide
A
A7/G
D/F#
Dm/F
A/E
A
w/o slide
w/ slide
w/o slide
1/2
1/2
w/ slide

# Traveling Riverside Blues

DAL 400 - 2

Words and Music by Robert Johnson

* Open A Tuning:
① = E ④ = E
② = C# ⑤ = A
③ = A ⑥ = E

**Intro**

**Moderately** ♩ = 95

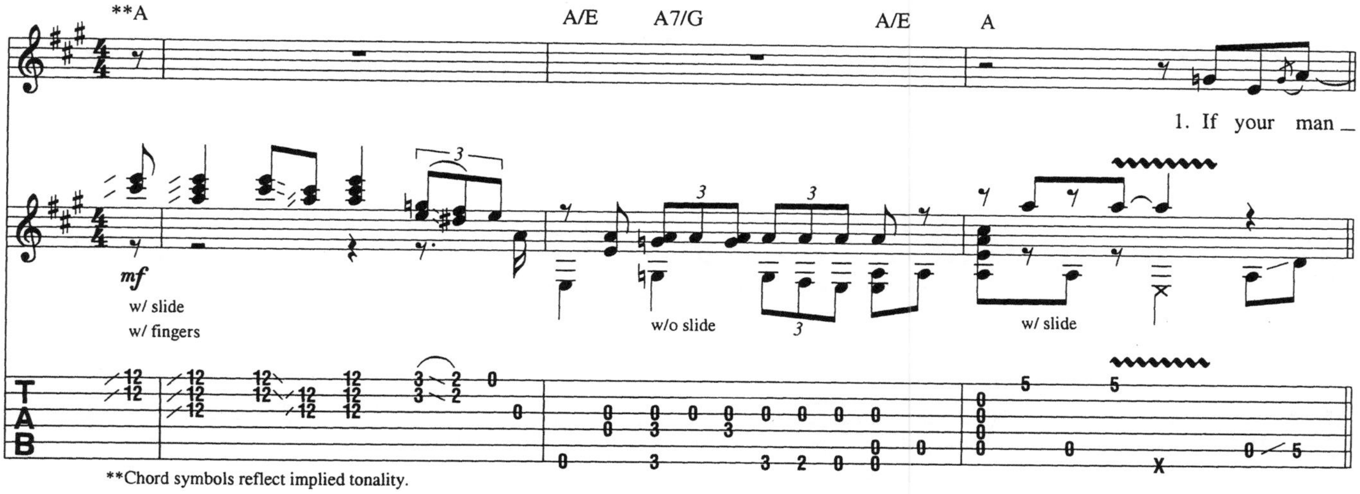

**A A/E A7/G A/E A

1. If your man

*mf*

w/ slide

w/ fingers

w/o slide

w/ slide

**Chord symbols reflect implied tonality.

**Verse**

D A

get per - son - al, want you to have your fun,

D

if your man get per - son - al,

w/o slide w/ slide w/o slide w/ slide

* Tunings were determined using the original 78s. To play along with the *Robert Johnson - The Complete Recordings* CD set, Capo I.
Editor's Note: In the re-tuning process, Robert's guitar progressively became sharper with each of the previous three songs until he became nearly 1/2 step sharp.

A
want you to have your fun,
w/o slide
w/ slide
w/o slide
w/ slide
D
just come on back to Fri - ar's Point, ma - ma, and bar - rel - house all night
A
long.
w/o slide
w/ slide
w/o slide
w/ slide
Verse
A
2. I got wom-ens in Vicks - burg, clean on in - to Ten - nes - see,

I got wom-ens
in Vicks-burg clean on in-to Ten-nes-see,
D
but my Fri-ars Point rid-er, now,
A
hops all o-ver me.
w/o slide
w/ slide

Verse
A
3. I ain't gon' to state no col-or, but her front teeth crowned with gold.
w/ slide
I ain't gon' to
w/ slide
w/o slide
w/ slide
w/o slide
w/ slide
state no col-or, but her front teeth is crowned with gold.
w/o slide
w/ slide
w/o slide
D
She got a mort - gage on my bod - y, now, and a
w/ slide
w/o slide
w/ slide
w/o slide
w/ slide

E
A
lien _ on my _ soul. ___
w/o slide
w/ slide
Verse
4. Lord, I'm _ go - in' to Rose - dale, gon - na take my
rid - er by my side. ___
Lord, I'm go - in' to Rose - dale gon' take my rid - er by _ my _ side. ___

We can still
w/o slide
w/ slide
D
barrel-house, baby, 'cause it's on the riv-er-side.
A
5. Now, you can squeeze
Verse
my lem-on 'til the juice run down my...
Spoken: 'til the juice run down

my leg, baby. You know what I'm talkin' 'bout. You can squeeze my lem-on 'til the
w/ slide
w/o slide
w/ slide
juice run down _ my leg. ___ Spoken: That's what I'm talkin' 'bout, now.
w/o slide
w/ slide
w/o slide
w/ slide
w/o slide
w/ slide
D
But I'm go-in' ___ back to Fri-ar's _ Point, if I be rock - in' _ to my head. ___
A7/G
D/F#
Dm/F
A/E
A
w/o slide
w/ slide

# Honeymoon Blues

DAL 401 - 1

Words and Music by Robert Johnson

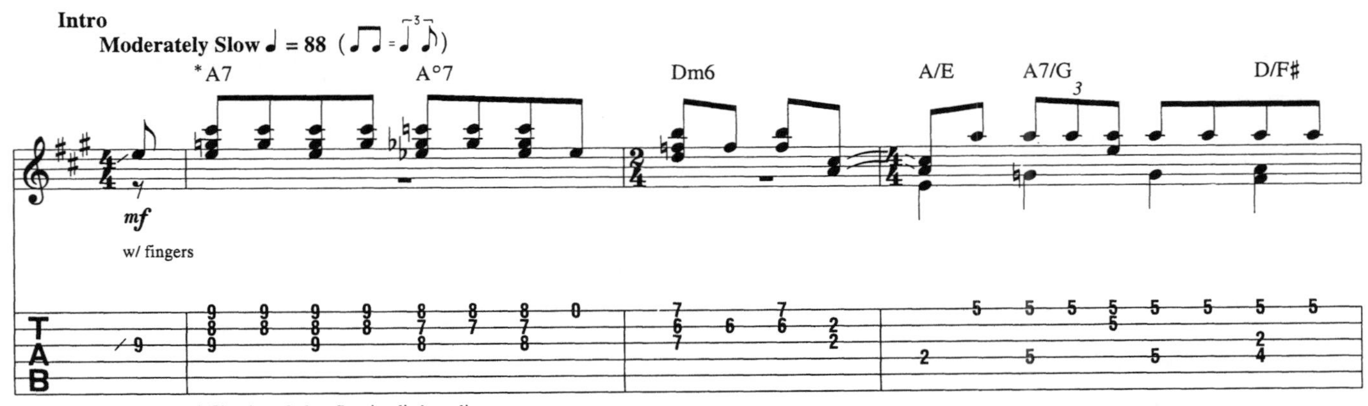


* Chord symbols reflect implied tonality.

* downstemmed notes only except during the turnarounds

Tunings were determined using the original 78s. To play along with the *Robert Johnson - The Complete Recordings* CD set, Capo I.

Editor's Note: In the retuning process, Robert's guitar became 1/4 step sharp for this recording.

D7/F#
A7
you shall be my wife some - day.
I wants a
E7
D/F#
lit - tle sweet girl
that will do an - y - thing that I say.
A A7/G D/F# Dm/F A/E E7
Verse
A7
2. Bet - ty Mae, you is my heart - string.
A°7 Dm6 A A7
You is my des - ti - ny.
Bet - ty Mae,

D7/F#
you is my heart - string.
You is my des - ti - ny.
A7
E7
A7
E7
And you rolls da - cross my mind, ba -
D7/F#
A
A7/G
D/F#
Dm/F
A/E
E7
by, each and ev - 'ry day.
3. Li'l girl,
Verse
A7
A°7
li'l girl,
my life seem so mis - e - ry.

A7
D7/F#
Hmm, mmm, lit - tle girl,
my life seem so mis - e - ry.
A7
E7
A7
Ba - by, I
E7
D/F#
guess it must be love, now, hoom - mmm Lord, that's tak - in' ef - fect on me.
A/E
A7/G
D/F#
Dm/F
A/E
E7
Verse
A7
4. Some day I will re - turn with the

A°7
Dm6
A
Dm6
A°7
A7
Dm6
A
mar - riage li - cense in my hand.
Some day I
D7/F#
A7
will re - turn,
hoo, hoo, 'th a mar-riage li-cense in my hand.
E7
A7
E7
I'm 'on' take you for a hon-ey - moon
D7/F#
A/E
A7/G
D/F#
Dm/F
E7
A7
in some long, long, dis-tant land.

# Love in Vain Blues

DAL 402 - 1

Words and Music by Robert Johnson

* Tunings were determined using the original 78s.
Editor's Note: In the re-tuning process, Robert's guitar progressively became sharper in pitch with each of the previous five songs until he became nearly 1/2 step sharp.

D7
G7/F
C/E
Cm/E♭
D7
when all your love's in vain.
All my love's in vain.
2. When the
Verse
G
G7
train rolled up to the sta - tion,
I looked her in the eye.
C
When the train rolled up to the sta - tion
and I looked her in the eye.
G7
D7
G
A7
Well, I was lone-some, I felt so lone-some

D7
G
G7/F
C/E
Cm/E♭
D
and I could not help but cry.
All my love's in vain.
3. When the
Verse
G
G7
train, it left the sta - tion
with two lights on be - hind.
C
When the train, it left the sta - tion
with two lights on be - hind.
G7
D7
G
A7
* even
Well, the blue light was my blues
* Sung and played as even eighth notes.

D7
G G7/F C/E Cm/E♭ D7
and the red light was my mind. All my love's in vain. 4. Ou,
Verse
G G7
hou, hoo, Wil-lie Mae. Oh,
C G D7 G
oh, hey, hoo, Wil-lie Mae. Ou,
A7 D7 G G7/F C/E Cm/E♭ G/D D7 G
ou, ou, ou, hee, vee, oh woe. All my love's in vain.

# Milkcow's Calf Blues

DAL 403 - 3

Words and Music by Robert Johnson

* Tunings were determined using the original 78s.
Editor's Note: In the re-tuning process, Robert's guitar progressively became sharper in pitch with each of the previous six songs until he became 1/2 step sharp.

A7
what on earth is wrong with you?
Now, you
E7
have a lit - tle new calf,
oo,
D7
and your milk is turn - in' blue.
w/ slide
A7
Verse
A7
2. Now your calf is hun - gry.
w/o slide
I be - lieve he needs a suck.
Now, your

D7
calf is hun - gry.
Hoo, I be-lieve he needs a suck.
1/4
A7
E7
But your milk is turn-in' blue. Hoo,
w/ slide
I be-lieve he's out - ta luck.
w/o slide
* Strike bridge with heel of right hand.
Bridge
Now I feel like milk-in' and my cow won't come.
I feel like chu'n-in' and my

D7
milk won't turn. _ I'm cry - in' plea - ease, plea - ease, don't do me wrong. _
A7
E7
If you see my milk cow, ba-by now, -
w/ slide
D7
A7
how, _ please drive _ her home. 3. My
w/o slide
Verse
A7
milk cow been ram - blin', hoo, - hee, _ for miles _ a - round. _
* Strike bridge with heel of right hand.

D7
My milk cow's been ram - blin',
* Strike bridge with heel of right hand.
A7
hoo, for miles a - round.
Well,
E7
D7
now she been suck - in' some oth - er man's bull cow,
hoo in this strange man's town.
w/ slide
w/o slide
A7
A7/G
D/F#
Dm/F
A/E
A
w/ slide

# Guitar Notation Legend

Guitar Music can be notated three different ways: on a *musical staff*, in *tablature*, and in *rhythm slashes*.

**RHYTHM SLASHES** are written above the staff. Strum chords in the rhythm indicated. Use the chord diagrams found at the top of the first page of the transcription for the appropriate chord voicings. Round noteheads indicate single notes.

**THE MUSICAL STAFF** shows pitches and rhythms and is divided by bar lines into measures. Pitches are named after the first seven letters of the alphabet.

**TABLATURE** graphically represents the guitar fingerboard. Each horizontal line represents a a string, and each number represents a fret.

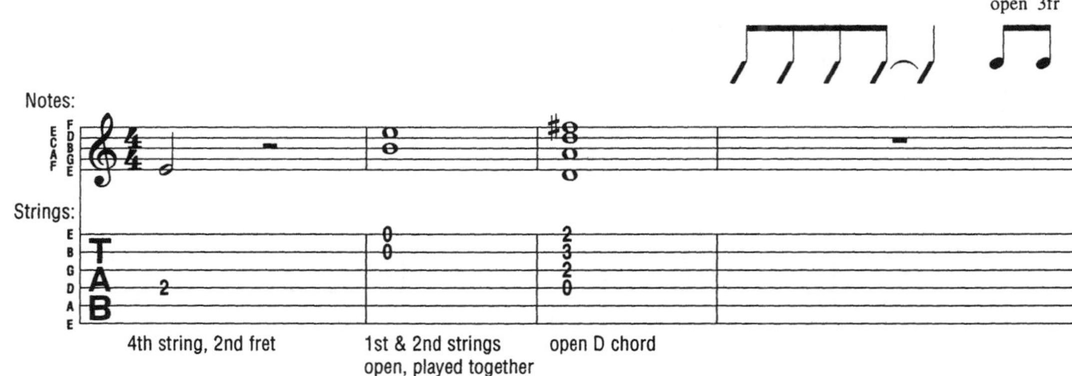


# Definitions for Special Guitar Notation

**HALF-STEP BEND:** Strike the note and bend up 1/2 step.

**WHOLE-STEP BEND:** Strike the note and bend up one step.

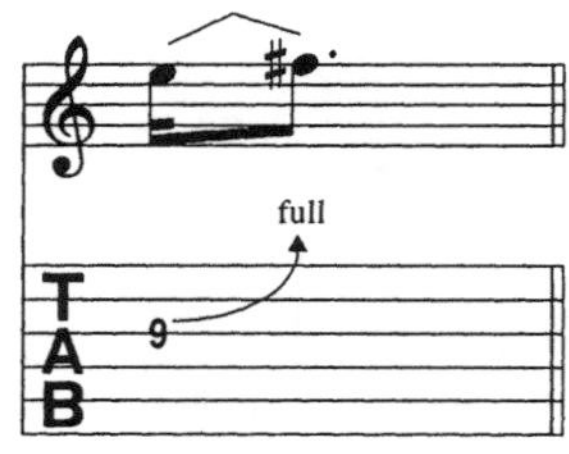


**GRACE NOTE BEND:** Strike the note and bend up as indicated. The first note does not take up any time.

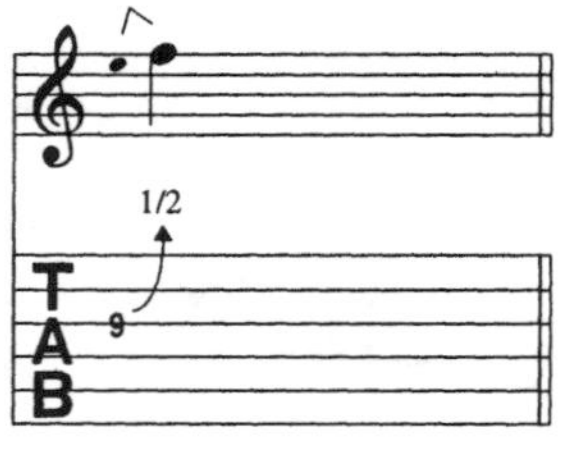


**SLIGHT (MICROTONE) BEND:** Strike the note and bend up 1/4 step.

**BEND AND RELEASE:** Strike the note and bend up as indicated, then release back to the original note. Only the first note is struck.

**PRE-BEND:** Bend the note as indicated, then strike it.

**PRE-BEND AND RELEASE:** Bend the note as indicated. Strike it and release the bend back to the original note.

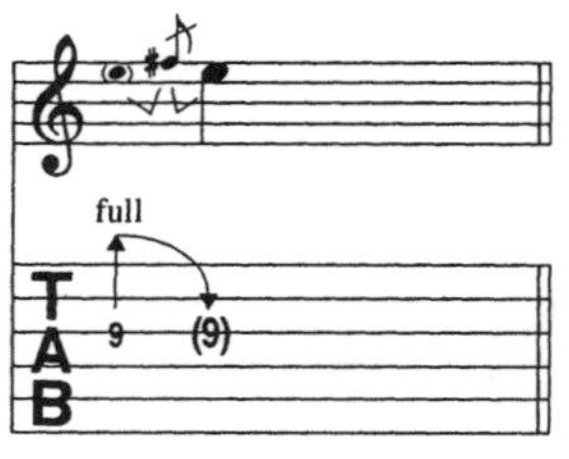


**UNISON BEND:** Strike the two notes simultaneously and bend the lower note up to the pitch of the higher.

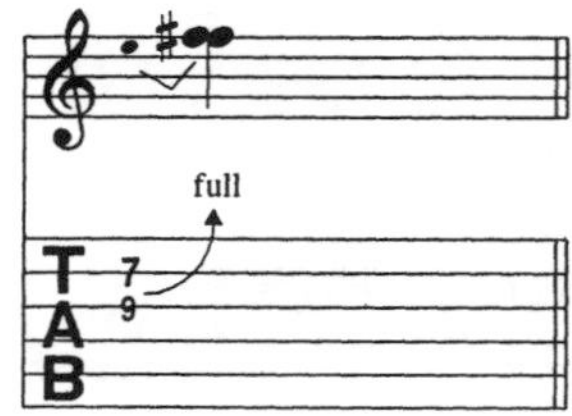


**VIBRATO:** The string is vibrated by rapidly bending and releasing the note with the fretting hand.

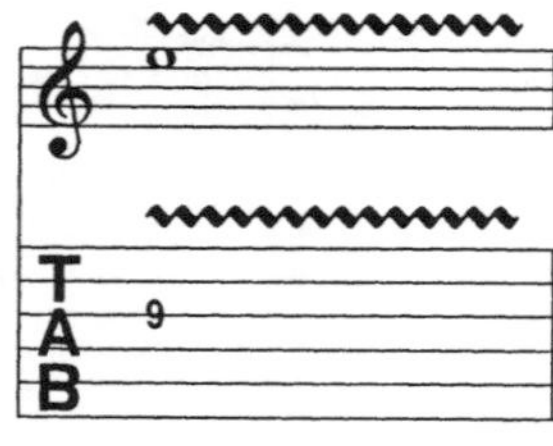

**WIDE VIBRATO:** The pitch is varied to a greater degree by vibrating with the fretting hand.

**HAMMER-ON:** Strike the first (lower) note with one finger, then sound the higher note (on the same string) with another finger by fretting it without picking.

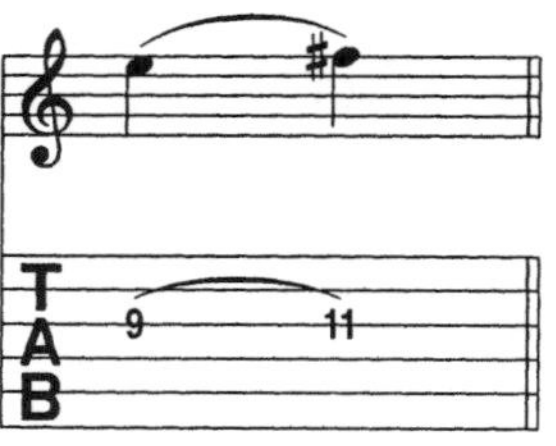

**PULL-OFF:** Place both fingers on the notes to be sounded. Strike the first note and without picking, pull the finger off to sound the second (lower) note.

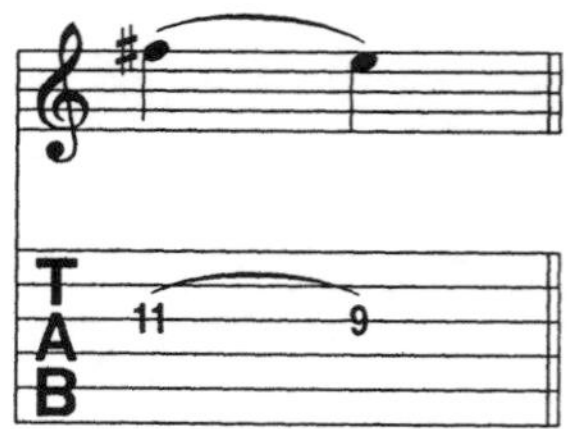

**LEGATO SLIDE:** Strike the first note and then slide the same fret-hand finger up or down to the second note. The second note is not struck.

**SHIFT SLIDE:** Same as legato slide, except the second note is struck.

**TRILL:** Very rapidly alternate between the notes indicated by continuously hammering on and pulling off.

**TAPPING:** Hammer ("tap") the fret indicated with the pick-hand index or middle finger and pull off to the note fretted by the fret hand.

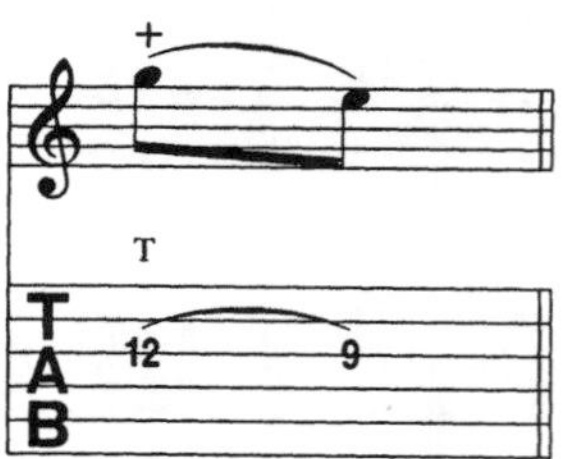

**IATURAL HARMONIC:** Strike the note while he fret-hand lightly touches the string lirectly over the fret indicated.

**PINCH HARMONIC:** The note is fretted normally and a harmonic is produced by adding the edge of the thumb or the tip of the index finger of the pick hand to the normal pick attack.

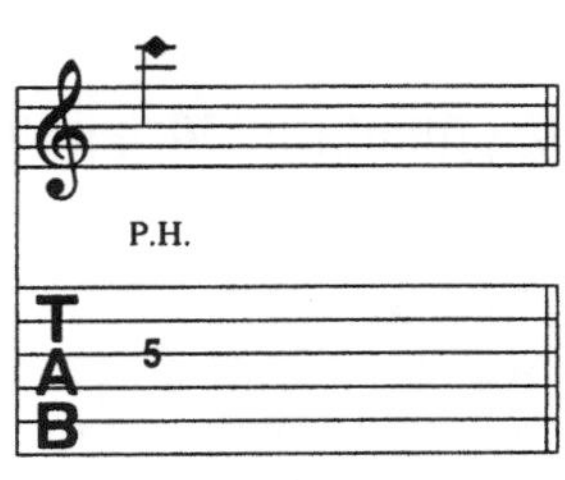


**HARP HARMONIC:** The note is fretted normally and a harmonic is produced by gently resting the pick hand's index finger directly above the indicated fret (in parentheses) while the pick hand's thumb or pick assists by plucking the appropriate string.

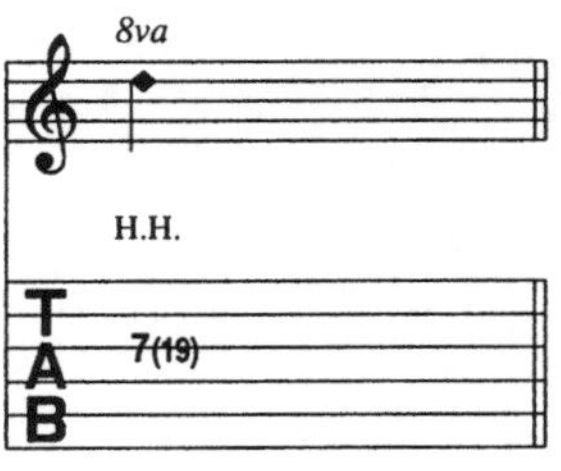


**PICK SCRAPE:** The edge of the pick is rubbed down (or up) the string, producing a scratchy sound.

**MUFFLED STRINGS:** A percussive sound is produced by laying the fret hand across the string(s) without depressing, and striking hem with the pick hand.

**PALM MUTING:** The note is partially muted by the pick hand lightly touching the string(s) just before the bridge.

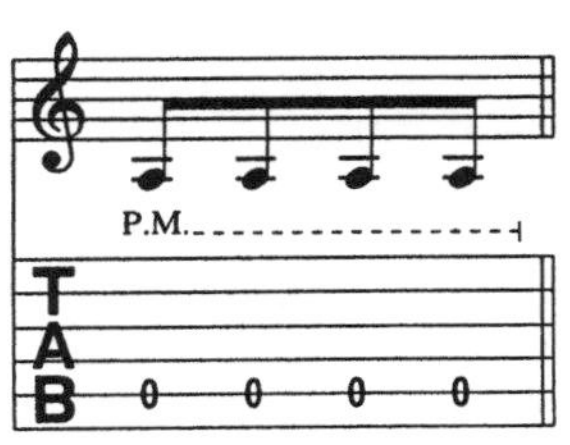


**RAKE:** Drag the pick across the strings indicated with a single motion.

**TREMOLO PICKING:** The note is picked as rapidly and continuously as possible.

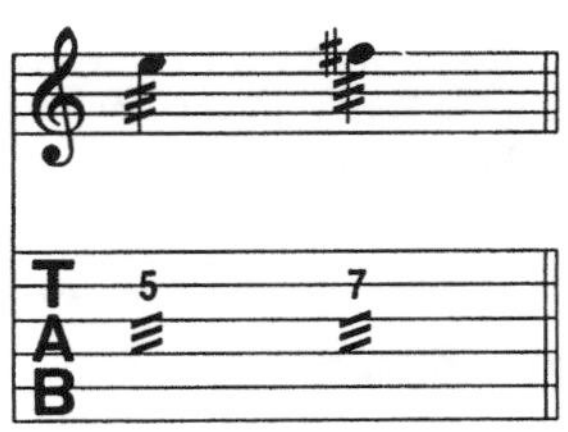


**ARPEGGIATE:** Play the notes of the chord indicated by quickly rolling them from bottom to top.

**VIBRATO BAR DIVE AND RETURN:** The pitch of the note or chord is dropped a specified number of steps (in rhythm) then returned to the original pitch.

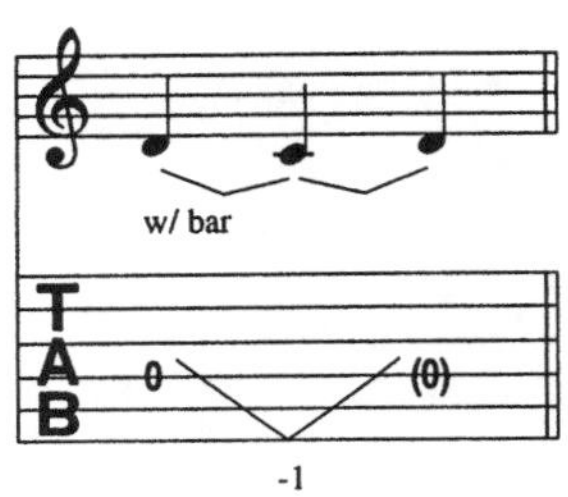


**VIBRATO BAR SCOOP:** Depress the bar just before striking the note, then quickly release the bar.

**VIBRATO BAR DIP:** Strike the note and then immediately drop a specified number of steps, then release back to the original pitch.

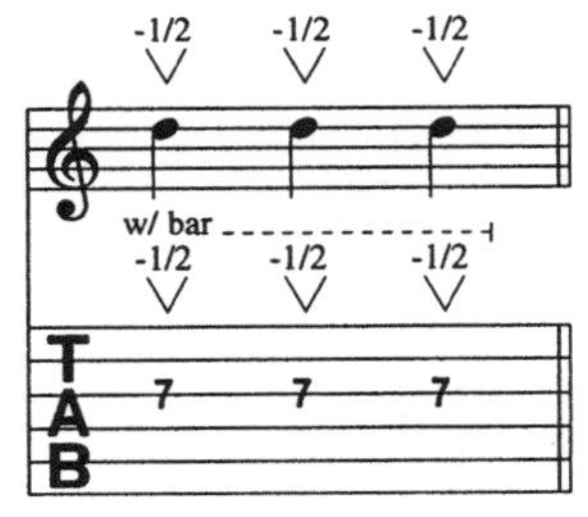


# Additional Musical Definitions

| | | | |
|---|---|---|---|
| 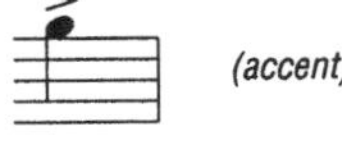 *(accent)* | • Accentuate note (play it louder) | **Rhy. Fig.** | • Label used to recall a recurring accompaniment pattern (usually chordal). |
| *(accent)* | • Accentuate note with great intensity | **Riff** | • Label used to recall composed, melodic lines (usually single notes) which recur. |
| *(staccato)* | • Play the note short | **Fill** | • Label used to identify a brief melodic figure which is to be inserted into the arrangement. |
| ⊓ | • Downstroke | **Rhy. Fill** | • A chordal version of a Fill. |
| V | • Upstroke | tacet | • Instrument is silent (drops out). |
| ***D.S. al Coda*** | • Go back to the sign ( 𝄋 ), then play until the measure marked "***To Coda***," then skip to the section labelled "***Coda***." | | • Repeat measures between signs. |
| ***D.S. al Fine*** | • Go back to the beginning of the song and play until the measure marked "***Fine***" (end). | 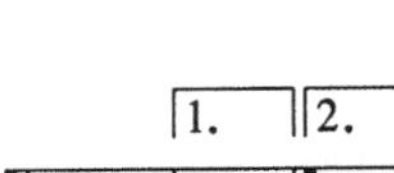  1. 2. | • When a repeated section has different endings, play the first ending only the first time and the second ending only the second time. |

**NOTE:** Tablature numbers in parentheses mean:
1. The note is being sustained over a system (note in standard notation is tied), or
2. The note is sustained, but a new articulation (such as a hammer-on, pull-off, slide or vibrato begins, or
3. The note is a barely audible "ghost" note (note in standard notation is also in parentheses).